🝗🝗🝗🝗🝗

THE CRACK IN THE TEACUP

🝗🝗🝗🝗🝗

THE MIRROR OF BRITAIN SERIES

THE MIRROR OF BRITAIN SERIES
General Editor : Kevin Crossley-Holland

THE CRACK
IN THE TEACUP

🔲🔲🔲🔲🔲

BRITAIN IN THE 20th CENTURY

🔲🔲🔲🔲🔲

Marina Warner

ANDRE DEUTSCH

For Roy

First published 1979 by
André Deutsch Limited
105 Great Russell Street London WCI

Set, printed and bound in Great Britain by
Fakenham Press Limited
Fakenham, Norfolk

Colour plates originated by
Keene Engraving Ltd, London
and printed by The White Quill Press Ltd
Mitcham, Surrey

British Library Cataloguing in Publication Data

Warner, Marina
  The crack in the teacup – (The mirror of
  Britain series).
  1. Great Britain – Civilization – 20th century
  – Juvenile literature
  941.082   DA566.4

  ISBN 0–233–96940–3

The glacier knocks in the cupboard,
The desert sighs in the bed,
And the crack in the teacup opens
A lane to the land of the dead.

W. H. AUDEN

🅖🅖🅖🅖🅖🅖

ACKNOWLEDGEMENTS

🅖🅖🅖🅖🅖🅖

Acknowledgement is due to the following for permission to reproduce the colour and black and white photographs: Berenice Abbott and the Marlborough Gallery, New York, 23; Francis Bacon and the Van Abbemuseum, Eindhoven, 9; Bill Brandt, 6; British Broadcasting Corporation, 50; British Library, 5, 11, 44; Colonel Henry Cotton, 4; E. R. Dodds, 39; EMI, 52; The Epstein Estate and the Beaverbrook Art Gallery, Canada, 17; Fitzwilliam Museum, 12; Mrs. Angelica Garnett, 2; Greater London Council, 46; Illustrated London News, 19; Imperial War Museum, 1, 7, 13, 15, 16, 18, 36; Romilly John, 24; Dan Jones, 8; A. F. Kersting, 47, 48; Kettles Yard, Cambridge, 21; Knoedler Gallery, 11; Jorge Lewinski, 53; London Transport, 3; Manchester City Art Gallery, 32, 42; Raymond Mander and Joe Mitchenson Theatre Collection, 27, 51; National Portrait Gallery, 7, 20, 25, 31, 45; Wilfred Owen Estate, 14; Penguin Books Ltd, 33; Popperphoto, 34; Punch, 35; Radio Times Hulton Picture Library, 1, 8, 9, 10; Rank Organization Ltd, 49; Lady Ritchie, 26; Roy Export Company Establishment, 28; Science Museum, 29a, 29b; Sotheby Parke Bernet, 38; Sothebys Belgravia, 37; Tate Gallery, 3, 10, 40, 41, 43; Times Newspapers Ltd, 2; Mrs Nancy Vernède, 30; Victoria and Albert Museum, 22; Mrs. G. A. Wyndham Lewis and The Durban Art Gallery, 5; Anne and Michael Yeats and the Sligo County Library and Museum, 4. Thanks are also owed to Horst Kolo for photographing plates 2, 26 and 33; to John Webb for photographing 6 and 10, to W. Anderson-Porter for photographing plate 8 and to the National Film Archive for supplying stills for plates 28, 49 and 52.

Grateful acknowledgement is due for permission to reprint extracts from the following works: W. H. Auden: 'In Memory of W. B. Yeats' and 'As I Walked Out One Evening' from *Collected Poems*; 'A Happy New Year' and 'A Communist to Others' from *The English Auden* by permission of Faber and Faber Ltd. Samuel Beckett: *Waiting for Godot* by permission of Faber and Faber Ltd and Grove Press Inc., New York. Julian Bell: 'Arms and the Man' from *New Signatures*, ed. by M. Roberts, by permission of Quentin Bell and the Hogarth Press. Joseph Conrad: *The Secret Agent* by permission of the Trustees of the Joseph Conrad Estate. Keith Douglas: *From Alamein to Zem Zem* (Oxford University Press) by permission of J. C. Hall and 'How to Kill' from *The Complete Poems* of Keith Douglas, ed. by Desmond Graham, © OUP 1978, by permission of Oxford University Press. T. S. Eliot: 'The Hollow Men' and 'The Waste Land' from *Collected Poems 1909–1962* by permission of Faber and Faber Ltd.

🔯🔯🔯🔯🔯

CONTENTS

🔯🔯🔯🔯🔯

ꗈꗈꗈꗈꗈꗈ

FOREWORD

ꗈꗈꗈꗈꗈꗈ

HISTORY is always in the making: even the story of the Middle Ages is remade each time it is seen again with new eyes. The process of understanding any time and any people is always to some extent creative. The history of the twentieth century, above all, must necessarily be subjective since distance has not yet placed events in perspective. I think it is quite likely that important events and discoveries have not yet emerged in their true definition, in the same way as the full effect of translating the Bible into the vernacular could not be known until after the Reformation. It is also likely that some of the century's greatest artists may be alive and unacknowledged, as Blake was in his own day, and Rembrandt towards the end of his life. So *The Crack in the Teacup* is full of choices and opinions and judgements and omissions which I realize are perhaps arbitrary and certainly selective. They might also turn out to be wrong. But I could not see any impartial or comprehensive way to write a short book about the interaction of art and politics in the British Isles today.

I have quoted passages rather than lines of prose and poetry, because often the special interest of twentieth century writing lies in the style of the authors, in their choice of syntax and vocabulary. There are, for instance, a myriad different theatrical modes of expression today, but Samuel Beckett has his unique tone of voice. It is impossible to have any impression of a modern writer – to feel Conrad's intensity or Wells' wit – without citing them at some length.

I could not have written this book without Dr R. F. Foster's guidance and bibliographical help, so my heartfelt thanks to him.

I am also grateful to Pam Royds for her editorial guidance and to Polly Dunnett for her skilful and patient picture research. The comments of Caspar Henderson were valuable indeed, and rescued me from important pitfalls.

ﾐﾐﾐﾐﾐﾐ

THE FAST CENTURY

ﾐﾐﾐﾐﾐﾐ

IF you had fallen asleep as Queen Victoria's long funeral pro-
cession wound round London in January, 1901, and only now,
some eighty years later, shaken yourself awake, you would not
think you were still in the same city, in the same country, in the
same world. You might be alarmed, you might be shocked, you
might be excited, even delighted by life as it unrolled before you
in its utterly changed aspect. You would certainly not be bored.
Everything you had known before, from the appearance of people
to the very texture of the road surface would be altered. The
twentieth century has seen the most violent upheavals and radical
transformations of any era in man's memory. In a remarkably
brief space of time the very substance of existence in Britain has
undergone no less than a revolution. She has ceased to be a major
power; but in many ways, she is a more progressive nation.

Discoveries, inventions, and, principally, technological inno-
vations have been responsible for the huge changes in society.
Although flight was achieved in 1903 – by the Wright brothers,
who flew for 12 seconds over sand dunes in North Carolina – it
was not until 1909 that the Channel was crossed – by the Frenchman, Blériot (see plate 1); and not until 1919 that Alcock and
Brown flew the North Atlantic. The aeroplanes that thunder into
Heathrow, Gatwick and Luton by the score every hour were only
visions in the wild minds of science fiction writers. Concorde
(see plate 2) can now cross the Atlantic in three hours. The same
journey took Alcock and Brown sixteen hours twelve minutes.
Yet the man who designed Concorde, Barnes Wallis, was already
22 years old when that historic first flight took place. These leaps

1. Humanity's long dream of flight came to pass in the twentieth century, and England's state as an island accessible only by sea was changed for ever. The Channel was first flown by Louis Blériot, above, in a monoplane in 1909.

into a dream future have taken place in the short space of a man's lifetime.

By 1900, the car had also been invented, but motoring was an enterprise for the rich alone, rather as private helicopters are today. Oil, the staple necessary for machine-travel, was sent for chemical analysis only in 1900, by one of the founders of Shell. Traffic was mainly horse-drawn carriages (see plate 3). Not a single motorway carved across the landscape; country roads had often not seen tarmac; in the cities, the streets were often still cobbled. Travel took place chiefly by train, for England in 1901 was cobwebbed with railway lines that could take passengers from small town to village in a way that is impossible today, when so

2. This is the fast century, when records have been established only to be broken. Concorde was designed by an Englishman, built by French and English aeronautical engineers, and is the fastest passenger plane in service, cruising at just under 1400 mph, a little over twice the speed of sound.

3. Traffic is a new phenomenon: Piccadilly Circus, London, at the turn of the century was almost free of the buses, lorries, taxis, vans, cars and motorcycles that now transport people and goods farther and faster than ever before.

many branch lines have been closed down. The bicycle was becoming popular. Freight was carried by wagon and horse. The juggernaut lorry did not exist.

Travelling was not undertaken with the casual ease of today. In the early years of the century, a family might migrate in search of employment, or have an outing by the seaside on a summer's day – but these were special expeditions, organized with care. Only the rich, commuting from one country house to another in pursuit of the pleasures they had invented for themselves and preserved and perfected over the centuries, used to travel without thinking much of it, as they summered in Norfolk or Sussex and wintered in Scotland, following the calendar of sporting events, shooting pheasant, grouse and deer, and playing cards and word-games over large teas.

The telephone, again, had already been invented, and the gramophone; but again it was the rich alone who used them. The majority of the population did not even have gas to fuel their heating or their cooking, let alone access to the complex electricity needed to work a telephone. Voices travelled down wires – that still seems miraculous enough. The greater wonder, the radio or 'wireless', had not yet been perfected, although Marconi and others had discovered the theory of air waves and were working to apply it. Marconi first succeeded in broadcasting in 1910.

No radio, so no television. Photography had already become an art, used for portraiture and social documentation under Victoria; and the 'moving picture', the cinema, also existed, though it had to wait till the First World War to attain its huge popularity. But television, the small cinema in every home, had not yet even been imagined – not even by the fertile romancer Jules Verne who prophesied flight and submarines and international fast travel.

There was almost no income tax – it was raised from 8 pence in the pound to a shilling in 1900. Gold sovereigns were in daily circulation. There were no passports: Englishmen could come and go as they pleased, if they could afford it, or if they wanted to emigrate – an attractive alternative to the difficulties of a working life in Britain. In 1911–13 there was a record exodus of English people. There were no immigration controls either: anyone who wished could come – until 1905 when a law was passed to restrict the entry of refugee Jews from Eastern Europe.

This Britain, which contained just over half the people of today – 37 million in England, Wales and Scotland according to the census of 1901, 40 million in 1911 – this Britain ruled a fifth of the world's population. When Queen Victoria was Empress of India (a title she liked for its connotations of power and romance) British dominions coloured half the globe red. The Empire included: a continent – Australasia; two subcontinents – India and Canada; huge portions of Africa – Ghana, Nigeria, Rhodesia, and countries which have realigned their borders and retaken African names – former Tanganyika and Nyasaland. Parts of Asia were ruled by British officials too – Burma, Malaya, Ceylon. Where Britain did not rule, it influenced profoundly through trade: in China, in America. British goods were carried all over the world. The country controlled half the world's trade in cotton goods; produced half the world's tonnage in ships; and in 1914 still owned 31 per cent of the entire global manufacturing trade. British ships were intrepid, far-travelling and practical. John Masefield described the commercial cargoes of the world's most highly industrialized country very well in his verse:

> Dirty British coaster with a salt-caked smokestack,
> Butting through the channel in the mad March days,
> With a cargo of Tyne coal,
> Road-rail, pig-lead,
> Firewood, iron-ware, and cheap tin trays.

But this Britain of 1901, so powerful, rich and self-assured, on which the fortunes of so many peoples rested, in whose charge lay the destinies of so many nations, was not a prosperous, comfortable, generous or healthy place for the men and women who lived in it. It tolerated poverty and squalor without feeling, it exacted work without sparing, it considered normal a chronic state of poor health amongst its population. Britain in 1901 was the equivalent of an underdeveloped country in such a critical condition that nowadays the relief agencies of the world would be mounting huge campaigns to work there. And it was in this state not for lack of cars or radio or television – progress has had little to do with them – but because individuals had no helping hand in the war against poverty and disease and weakness and penury. For theirs was a very unequal fight: all the economic forces which concentrated power in the hands of employers and made competition cut-throat tended to rub out the individual, 'the little man'.

The Edwardian age lasted from the death of Queen Victoria to the outbreak of the First World War (although King Edward VII, after whom it was named, died in 1910). It has often been regarded as the gentle, delightful twilight of England's last period of greatness. This is not altogether accurate. Society then was highly structured, often bleak, often harsh. So for the Edwardian, what was it like to live then, when everything was so different?

ඕඕඕඕඕඕ

LAND OF HOPE AND GLORY

ඕඕඕඕඕඕ

> How strange that eating should play so important a part in
> social life! They were eating quails and cracking jokes. That
> particular dish of the Chevron chef was famous: an ortolan
> within the quail, a truffle within the ortolan, and pâté de
> foie gras within the truffle . . . From his place at the head
> of the table, Sebastian watched the jaws going up and down,
> and wished that he did not always see people as though they
> were caricatures. . . . Fourteen down one side of the table,
> fourteen up the other . . . the jewels glittered; the shirt-
> fronts glistened; the servants came and went . . .
>   VITA SACKVILLE-WEST *The Edwardians*

BRITAIN for the Edwardian represented the norm of civilized
society. In spite of the access officials of the Empire had to people
of other races and creeds, British customs and attitudes remained
the ones any decent person should adopt, or so it seemed. Men
and women who lived in India, or in Burma, administering
British justice and imposing British ways of life on other nations
tried to maintain a separate style of life; the phrase 'going native',
which meant living like an Indian, or like a Burmese, spoke of
depths of horror (see plate 4). There was no doubt in the mind of
most Edwardians that the British way was best.

British rule brought many of the benefits of technical advance
to its subject states: in the rest of Asia there is no transport to com-
pare with the railways of India, laid out by the British. But the
advantages of law and trade that Britain brought were spoiled by
the thick-skinned belief that the Englishman was better than anyone else. Rudyard Kipling (1865–1936) epitomizes the attitudes

4. Life under the Raj – British rule in India – carried on English social traditions like afternoon tea as nostalgic rituals to recall the home that had been left behind.

of the Edwardian era, the era of unselfconscious paternalism (see plate 5). He was born in Bombay and spent his early life working in India. The experience set alight an already bright imagination and a skilful sense of narrative which made him one of the greatest romancers and tale-tellers in the English language. Through his many stories and novels, his large volume of verse, Kipling evokes accurately the domination of Britain in his day, and the authority of the white man in India. *Kim* (1901), one of his mostly widely read novels, is a characteristic Empire document. In spirited prose, it tells the story of a mischievous young boy who runs wild in the Indian bazaars as a Hindu waif-and-stray, until he discovers that he is the child of an Irish soldier. This makes him a white Sahib, or master, and completely alters his status in Indian society. He is taken to be educated as a British boy and then, back in Indian costume, used to spy for the British on the internal affairs of the country. The mixture of different

5. Rudyard Kipling, photographed here for the *Tatler* while on holiday in 1912, was a great poet and storyteller of Empire, with a wide knowledge of Indian lore.

religious sects, each with a different way of life, set in the teeming street-life of India, is presented as a great colourful frieze. Excitement and exotica, spice and fun are all mixed up together. Meanwhile British officialdom effortlessly keeps order from on high. *Kim* presents a very simplified and romantic view, completely lacking in compassion, of one of the greatest civilizations that England sought to dominate. Yet it has remained a popular book, because it covers up all the difficulties of imperial administration, and turns into easy picturesque adventure the problems that in the end spelt out the partial failure of British justice overseas.

Foreign parts, viewed from the England of the 1900s, were mysterious, wicked, barbarous places. Kipling was also aware of this attitude, and satirized it in his poem 'We and They':

> Father, Mother, and Me
> Sister and Auntie say
> All the people like us are We,
> And everyone else is They.
> And They live over the sea,
> While We live over the way,
> But – would you believe it? – They look upon We
> As only a sort of They! . . .
>
> We shoot birds with a gun.
> They stick lions with spears.
> Their full dress is un-.
> We dress up to Our ears. . . .

The Edwardians kept their fathers' relish for tales which revealed the rest of the world's fascinating abnormality. The literature of the turn of the century is full of enthralling escapades in which sober Englishmen become involved with pagan doings, either in Africa, in the tradition of Rider Haggard's *King Solomon's Mines*, or in a fanciful central Europe, as in Anthony Hope's exciting concoctions *The Prisoner of Zenda* and *Rupert of Hentzau*. John Buchan, a writer of thrilling mysteries – *The Thirty-Nine Steps* is the most famous – commanded a huge audience for half a century. His stories of skulduggery and villainy take place in what is now a dated and highly snobbish framework. Dark foreigners are often the source of the mischief. One of the eminent literary men of the Edwardian era, Andrew Lang, lent his authority and talent to a collaboration with the yarn-spinner Rider Haggard on a costume drama story called *The World's Desire*, set in Ancient Egypt, with Ulysses and Helen as the heroes. The taste for adventure also liked the added spice of violence. The

Empire sensibility had a tough old hide. Kipling, again, caught its character perfectly in his famous ballad, addressed to an Indian army servant:

> Though I've belted you and flayed you,
> By the livin' Gawd that made you,
> You're a better man than I am, Gunga Din!

England's power always fascinated the Edwardians. Edward Elgar, a composer of flowing, lyrical melodies that often take their inspiration from the rolling contours of the English landscape, expressed the patriotic side of the Edwardian spirit in his most famous tune, the march 'Pomp and Circumstance' – 'Land of Hope and Glory'. It was only at this level, as self-glorifying propaganda, that British hegemony over the world entered the minds of English people. For all it affected the standard of living of the ordinary family in the 1900s, the Empire might well not have existed.

Britain was a narrow world, with its own hard and fast rules. The most important code of all concerned class. The chief ingredient in any man's personality, when assessed by anyone else at that time, was his social position – his class. Society was stratified very clearly and it was an expected form of behaviour for everyone, at each level, to lord it over anyone beneath. This hierarchical instinct sometimes took subtle forms – a gentleman would not for instance be rude to a servant – but it was deeply ingrained, so ingrained in fact that the inequality was considered inevitable, natural, insurmountable.

The class in power was the rich, often synonymous with the old landed aristocracy. When a man of humbler birth became rich through business and industry – not uncommon then and earlier – he usually copied the behaviour of the aristocracy, followed its traditions, and did not seek to change the customs of the upper classes. A successful factory-owner for instance would often bring up his son to pursue one of the 'gentlemanly' professions – the Empire, Politics, the Church – rather than let him remain in trade like his own father. So although Edwardian society was mobile, in the sense that some individuals did move up the social ladder, it was at the same time stagnant, because their advancement did not cause any ripple in the calm lake of Edwardian self-assurance.

The wealth was fabulous. There was hardly any tax, and no death duties. Estates passed intact from father to son. From the evidence of wills, it has been estimated that 1 per cent of the population over 25 owned 67 per cent of the wealth of the country; that is, about 180,000 people only were worth £4,400,000,000 between them. If one takes the top 13 per cent of the population, the picture does not become any more just: these rich people owned 92 per cent of the wealth, leaving a tiny 8 per cent to be divided among the millions of other people in England. The gap between rich and poor was wider than it had been since the days of serfs.

The life of the wealthy was pure pleasure, and was enjoyed openly, with conspicuous display. The King himself, Edward VII, personified the age: jolly, sensual, rough and ready when it came to anything like the appreciation of music and poetry. His aristocratic subjects were idle, fun-loving, hearty as himself; there was a widespread distrust of the arts, as if they were somehow unrespectable, and a corresponding confidence in the 'manly' pursuits: huntin', shootin', fishin'. The families of substance followed the racing season around Britain, for the Horse was in many ways the totem of their class, the symbol which united them. They loved sport, especially shooting. Kenneth Clark, the art historian, remembers in his autobiography how his father and friends would sometimes shoot over 1,000 pheasants in one afternoon. There are two novelists who have chronicled, from different ends, the structure of social life in Edwardian Britain. John Galsworthy (1867–1933) described the preoccupation with property and substance and style of the influential classes in his moral tableau *The Forsyte Saga*. His protagonist, Soames Forsyte, wishes to have everything that is considered desirable and respectable by others. The atmosphere of his establishment is suffocatingly discreet and conventional, yet the instincts which motivate him are greedy, ambitious, and fundamentally frivolous. *The Forsyte Saga* captures the easy-going materialism of the

Edwardians perfectly; and this picture of a vanished age of plenty has become pleasantly nostalgic for contemporary audiences. The television serial based on Galsworthy's novels was one of the most successful ever made, both in Britain and in America.

A novelist of greater stature and sensitivity who was also morally concerned with the values of his contemporaries is H. G. Wells (1866–1946), philosopher, scientist, committed social reformer. He looks at life from the bottom, rather than the top, and he can be very funny indeed, as well as serious. *Kipps* (1905) is a tragi-comic masterpiece about the horrors of class distinction and behaviour in Edwardian England. Inarticulate, lumpen, anxious-to-please Arthur Kipps inherits a fortune and so finds himself plummeted into the bewildering intricacies of high society. One of his worst ordeals is an Anagram Tea, a particular social trial during which each guest wears a jumbled word on his lapel which the other guests have to decipher. Kipps becomes quite terrified, and bolts.

Idleness was such a way of life that games were constantly used to while away the hours. Cards – bridge and poker especially – were widely played, always for money, and sometimes for very high stakes. The upper classes even played tennis for high bets on the hard courts coming into fashion. Nicknames were in vogue: Edwardians called each other Bongie, Whibbles, Bluetooth, Kakoo, Cis, Ickey, Goonie or Gan-Gan. In speech, words were altered according to a characteristic upper class inflexion: by adding 'ers' or 'aggers' to anything, so that Association Football for instance becomes 'soccer'. It was a golden time for the rich when whims could be indulged. Kenneth Clark also describes his eleventh birthday treat, in July, 1914:

> 'A row of mortars were dug into the grass in front of the house at Pool Ewe and into them were placed large but light cannon balls. The mortars were then discharged, the cannon balls shot up into the pale blue sky, and when they burst there emerged huge paper effigies which floated down like leisurely parachutes into the surrounding hills. Elephants, geishas (for of course, these wonderful toys came from Japan), tigers, buffaloes, slowly descending on to the distant heather . . .'

The arts survived in spite of the landed classes, traditionally their patrons, rather than because of them. Composers like Elgar, Ralph Vaughan Williams, and Delius added lyrical, sweeping and romantic power to the tradition of English music, but they survived through the energy of other musicians, like the conductor Thomas Beecham, who loved Delius above all contemporary composers. The vigorous Malcolm Sargent used his personal charm to bring music before the public and promote its importance in daily life. (But both Sargent and Beecham only became truly effective campaigners in the next two decades, with radio and gramophone records at their disposal.)

Society used portrait painters to commemorate its men of power and its women of beauty – artists like John Lavery. Occasionally a greater talent, like that of Augustus John, also found employment, but generally recognition was elusive, and it was only with the Twenties that a new appreciation of art developed. The Edwardians were Philistines, and the age was in many ways the last fling of the irresponsible rich. Many of them half-suspected it. They continued to revere the Victorian virtues, while failing to practise them. The society was gradually becoming more and more secularized, and church was a formality on Sundays for most Anglicans, rather than a felt faith. The Edwardian moral code was enshrined in Kipling's famous poem 'If –', which defines a true 'Man'. It paints the highest virtues. These have ceased to be Charity or Humility as Christ preached them, but a new morality which could be summed up as stiff upper lip. One verse begins:

> If you can make one heap of all your winnings
> And risk it on one turn of pitch-and-toss
> And lose, and start again at your beginnings
> And never breathe a word about your loss ...

The poem praises hard work, forbearance, patience, honesty, perseverance, stoicism, tolerance. All excellent qualities, but lacking a human dimension.

> If neither foes nor loving friends can hurt you,
> If all men count with you, but none too much ...

For many Edwardians, Kipling's poem replaced the catechism; yet they had largely stopped following its injunctions. They had become much fatter, sleeker and lazier than their Victorian predecessors.

Edwardian hedonism was only made possible by the work of others, less advantaged. Everything a rich man required was provided by servants. A country house, visited only once a year for a month at the right time of the shooting season, might need fifty servants to keep it up. For these enormous establishments were without gas, electricity or running water. Servants carried coal down long corridors, up long flights of stairs to each bedroom at dawn so that the room might be warm when the gentleman or lady rose; later they brought hot water up from the kitchen hob – so that they could wash in comfort. For a bath, several journeys with kettles and buckets had to be made. Edwardians of the upper class also ate prodigiously: sideboards at breakfast would be laden with hams, porridge, poached eggs, muffins, sausages, boiled plovers' eggs, tea, milk, coffee. They also dressed themselves elaborately, so that every lady needed a maid to help pull her stays tighter and button her up, and more servants behind the green baize door to wash, iron, crimp and goffer the starched and lacy undergarments and gowns she wore. She needed help to wash her long hair – never cut from birth – and dress it in the high, voluptuous styles of the period. The daughter of a woman who had been 'in service' remembered that one of her mother's employers, at the age of 30, had still never washed herself. Children too were waited upon: taught by governesses or sometimes private tutors, washed and walked and fed by maids. Forty-six per cent of the population – most of them women – worked in domestic situations in 1911 (see plate 6). For this they were poorly rewarded financially, and, at a broader level, emotionally. It was a life of complete poverty of spirit for most people. Even higher up the social scale, where domestic work was not the inevitable lot, life offered little hope. H. G. Wells makes the hero of his book, *The History of Mr Polly*, survey the bleak drudgery of his life in a shop and wonder where all his fine dreams went. From his meagre beginnings everything had been against him. Wells

6. A parlourmaid and an underparlourmaid wait for the family to come down to
dinner, in a household photographed by Bill Brandt in 1933 but unchanged since
Edwardian times.

describes the education available to lower middle class people
then:

> 'Mr Polly went into the National School at 6, and he left the private
> school at 14, and by that time his mind was in much the same state
> as you would be in, my dear reader, if you were operated on for
> appendicitis by a well-meaning, boldly enterprising, but rather over-
> worked and underpaid butcher boy, who was superseded at the
> climax of the operation by a left-handed clerk of high principles but
> intemperate habits – that is to say, it was a thorough mess.'

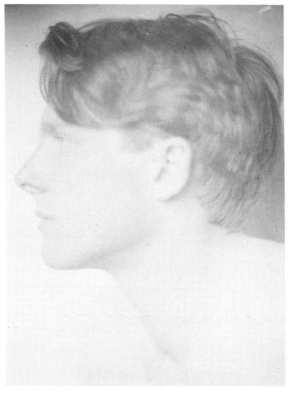

7. Rupert Brooke became one of the country's most widely read writers and a national hero after his death in the First World War.

The countryside was largely unspoilt, and from the gentle nature poetry characteristic of the time, one gets the impression that the countryside was a dominant joy in most people's lives, alleviating some of the hardships and the tedium. Yet more people lived in towns in Britain than in any other country. But England remained identified with rolling gentle green fields, hedgerows of wild flowers and birds' nests, birdsong in the mornings, glinting rivers and wild moors. When Rupert Brooke (see plate 7) recalled his homeland and spoke of

> Her sights and sounds, dreams happy as her days
> And laughter learned of friends, and gentleness
> In hearts at peace, under an English Heaven.

he evokes the countryside, punting on the river Cam to the village of Grantchester that he loved, walks in unspoilt woods, picnics in June sunshine. It is a twilight, bitter-sweet, soft-centred world. The leisured class, to which Brooke belonged, could use the country for their pastimes; but the workers increasingly drifted into the towns to find work.

The towns, especially the factory towns of the North, would not have inspired Rupert Brooke's lyricism. They were, in Wells's phrase 'pestilential heaps of rotten private property'. Life in them was harsh. The industrialist and philanthropist, Seebohm Rowntree, conducted a survey in York in 1901. He found that 28 per cent of the adult inhabitants were not eating enough to keep themselves in ordinary health; and that among the children, the figure was nearly 40 per cent. Most of the children rarely saw good meat or fresh fruit and vegetables. One woman interviewed recently remembered the hunger of her childhood: 'My mother

8. Slum conditions, such as this family were suffering in 1912, were so widespread before the First World War that barely half the men called up to fight enjoyed normal health.

9. Women, like these workers in a Manchester millinery factory in 1909, suffered from overcrowded and harsh surroundings. They provided half the work force in Britain, but were paid much less than the men.

went without herself for us, yes. I've known her wipe the plate round with a drop of gravy, and tell my father she'd had her dinner, she'd never had any.' (See plate 8). Childhood did not last as long as it does today, and education was soon over. At 14 the hunt for work began, and then the same bitter grind which the parents had undergone became the experience of the children.

The conditions of work were terrible. A few kindhearted employers here and there might help to improve the lot of their workers, but this was the exception, not the rule. There were few safeguards in law. The suffragette Hannah Mitchell, following a typical pattern of Edwardian youth, left her family's tiny farm to work as a seamstress in the northern mill town of Bolton, Lancs., for about 12 shillings a week. Many women in this situation worked 6 days a week, often till 9 or 10 at night (see plate 9). If

10. The boy here has been apprenticed in a workshop. Schooling ended for the majority at 14; work followed immediately, usually in grim and underpaid conditions.

there were customers waiting for dresses, the seamstress had to stay in to finish them. It was only in unionized labour – and only a fraction of the labour force was organized in unions – that a limit to working hours had been arranged.

Men, though always better-paid than women, were also worked very hard for poor wages – exploited, in our eyes today. At the age of 14, a boy could apply for an apprenticeship (see plate 10). H. G. Wells describes how Arthur Kipps gets a 'crib' or place in a draper's shop. The establishment provides him with food and lodging, in a dormitory above the premises, where he retires after a long day before an early rise. H. G. Wells began life himself as a draper's apprentice and so he describes Kipps' plight from personal knowledge, with bitterness and sarcasm. He cries out

1. With that bitter irony that characterizes much of the First World War's poetry, Paul Nash called his painting (above) of the tormented trench landscape in Flanders in 1918, *We Are Making A New World*.

2. Virginia Woolf, novelist and essayist of genius, the focal point of the Bloomsbury Group, painted by Duncan Grant in 1911.

3. Lytton Strachey, a mordant biographer and wit, was another member of the Group. His languid looks, characteristic of the movement's aestheticism, are well caught in Henry Lamb's painting.

for a remedy to the situation which stifles the Kippses of this world:

> The indentures that bound Kipps to Mr Shalford were antique and complex . . . they made him over, body and soul, to Mr Shalford for seven long years, the crucial years of life. In return there were vague stipulations about teaching the whole art and mystery of the trade to him, but as there was no penalty attached to negligence, Mr Shalford being a sound, practical, business man, considered this a mere rhetorical flourish, and set himself assiduously to get as much out of Kipps and to put as little into him as he could in the seven years of their intercourse.
>
> What he put into Kipps was chiefly bread and margarine, infusions of chicory and tea-dust, colonial meat by contract at threepence a pound, potatoes by the sack and watered beer. . . . He was also allowed to share a bedroom with eight other young men, and to sleep in a bed which, except in very severe weather, could be made, with the help of his overcoat and private underlinen, not to mention newspapers, quite sufficiently warm for any reasonable soul.

No one was ashamed of this kind of meanness, just as no one felt that schoolteachers who were free with the cane, as most were, should be taken to task for cruelty.

What softened the circumstances of the working man? Drink was his chief pleasure. Pubs stayed open all day, till midnight, and there were so many that it worked out at 1 for every 300 people. But drink could not stop the cities being overcrowded, poorly-lit, insanitary, and, in winter, very, very cold. Noise pollution is complained about now; but men now in their seventies remember when they were children how the streets rang and rumbled like timpani and cymbals together from the steel hoops of the wagon wheels bringing provisions to the big cities. Outside the hospitals, the cobbles were strewn with straw to muffle some of the roar. And the horses – there were 250,000 horses in London alone – needed provender and stabling, so the streets were ceaselessly swept of horse droppings in the better parts of town, by men who were tipped at crossings by pedestrians who could afford it.

After a lifetime of labour, an old man or woman could not expect much shelter in these grim towns. One of the greatest novelists of the century, Joseph Conrad (1857–1924), was born Polish, in the Ukraine, went to sea as a boy, but left the sailor's life in his thirties and settled in England to write. He became one of the most sensitive and enriching users of the language in novels that often centre on a man's struggle to overcome his innate weakness or the threat of external turmoil. In *Nostromo*, *Lord Jim* and *Typhoon*, amongst his most famous novels, he uses the setting of the ocean and exotic faraway places to unfold grand personal adventures; but in *The Secret Agent* (1907) one of his most obsessive and masterly books, he describes London, and provides a dark, even terrifying portrait of the meanness and squalor of the lives of the poor in that city. As usual in Conrad, the story is gripping, but he mingles the elements of a thriller with psychological insight and relentless examination of the forces that drive people. The mother of his heroine Winnie Verloc has decided to remove herself to an almshouse in favour of her children, so that she should not overburden her son-in-law's generosity. She has asked for charity help, and so she sets off, with her half-witted son and her oppressed daughter, to this last home. The scene of dismal misery in London catches the pitilessness of that period when a woman could expect very little in her old age. They drive off in a horse-drawn cab:

> ... she turned her old tearful eyes to the roof of the cab. Then she averted her head on the pretence of looking out of the window, as if to judge of their progress. It was insignificant, and went on close to the curbstone. Night, the early dirty night, the sinister, hopeless and rowdy night of South London, had overtaken her on her last cab drive. In the gas-light of the low-fronted shops her big cheeks glowed with an orange hue under a black and mauve bonnet. ...
>
> In the privacy of a four-wheeler, on her way to a charity cottage (one of a row) which by the exiguity of its dimensions and the simplicity of its accommodation, might well have been devised in kindness as a place of training for the still more straitened circumstances of the grave, she was forced to hide from her own child a blush of remorse and shame.

Winnie Verloc's mother was lucky that a philanthropist had set up these cottages at all; Edwardian old age could be even more bitter. One in five people who lived to the age of 70 died paupers, and if they managed 75 – a great age then for a working person – the figure became one in three.

But cracks were appearing in the edifice of the Edwardian World. It was not a permanent society. Classes, hitherto law-abiding and silent, took to violent methods to express their demands. Irish independence, women's right to vote, and workers' demands were all creating trouble. The Liberal Government under Asquith was pledged to give Ireland Home Rule – that is, independence from Westminster and an Irish Government in Dublin of all Ireland. But certain sections of the Tory opposition would not hear of this separation, and as an argument against it, they used the reluctance of the Protestant-dominated counties of the north-east – Ulster – to be subsumed under the 'papish' south. Some fine orators lent their voices to the cause of Ulster – an independent original like Sir Edward Carson, a southern Irish Protestant who had made a fortune at the English Bar, and was famous for his brutality with Oscar Wilde during the latter's trial; or a maverick like F. E. Smith, a brilliant speaker, and an ardent, witty but self-interested barrister and Tory politician. Tory support was whipped up: many opposition MPs saw Home Rule and its defeat as the issue that would bring down the Liberal Government; they did not stop to think what their unprincipled use of it for their own political ends might mean for Ireland and for England. Their enthusiasm lent courage to the men of Northern Ireland who wanted to remain under British rule. Quite illegally, they were organized into militia and drilled – with wooden rifles – by Sir Edward Carson, now in his element as a type of gentleman bandit. Everyone knew that soon those toys would be replaced by the real, murderous weapons themselves. So fanatical was the movement that one spokesman even threatened treachery, saying Ulster would prefer Germans to Irish as rulers.

Later, Sean O'Casey, an Irish working-class Protestant who was deeply involved in the Nationalist movement, wrote a powerful play, *The Plough and the Stars*, about the Irish tragedy. He set the action in Dublin during the Easter Rising of 1916 and with high drama and emotionalism counterpoints the intimate, family values of his heroine, Nora Clitheroe, with the patriotic sense of duty of her husband Jack. Jack goes to fight the English. The soldier who reports his death sums up for O'Casey the heartless fanaticism to which the Irish problem could lead:

> Captain Brennan: He took it like a man. His last whisper was to 'Tell Nora to be brave; that I'm ready to meet my God, an' that I'm proud to die for Ireland.' An' when our General heard it he said that 'Commandant Clitheroe's end was a gleam of glory.' Mrs Clitheroe's grief will be a joy when she realises that she had had a hero for a husband.

But Nora goes mad and in her madness, she attracts the attention of a sharpshooter and causes the death of the friend who gave her shelter as well as her own. O'Casey's play is occasionally melodramatic, and it plucks unrestrainedly at the heartstrings. Nevertheless it dramatizes with enduring importance the horror of this quarrel about Ireland and Ireland's position *vis-à-vis* England. The effects of the Tory opposition to Home Rule, and the illegal militarism used to enforce it, are with us still today in the civil strife of Ulster, the terrorism and the bombs, in London, Belfast and Derry.

Another class who, more surprisingly perhaps, resorted to violence and illegal means to win a hearing were women. Women in Edwardian Britain did not have the right to vote. The denial of their participation in English democracy was bad enough, but worse was that women's votelessness symbolized the view Edwardian manhood held: that women were mentally inferior, apt to hysterics, physically weak, and in general fit only to be looked after by their superiors. This attitude disregarded altogether the contribution of women to society: women were strong enough for factory work, but not strong enough to vote. They were intelligent enough to be entrusted with the rearing of children, one of the most critical tasks in any society, yet too weak in the head to think. The Edwardian lady was queen of the home, gracious, beautiful and good – only because she was untarnished by the dirt of the outside world of politics and business. The dream woman in man's eyes may as well have been a doll. The prejudice was a mass of contradictions; and its solidity seems almost unbelievable today. It could not be budged. Part of the trouble was women themselves, some of whom refused to see what emancipation might mean. The best-selling pulp novelist, Marie Corelli, was outspoken and obscurantist, arguing that women had hidden powers over men: 'If she is a real Woman with the mystic power to persuade, enthral and subjugate man, she has no need to come down from her throne and mingle in any of his political frays.'

Some members of the Liberal Government were however pledged to give women the vote; again they wavered and weakened until it became obvious to the suffragists – the campaigners for the vote – that the Government was going to let the issue slide in the face of the mass hostility of the people. So the suffragettes, led by a formidable trio, Mrs Emmeline Pankhurst and her fiery daughters Christabel and Sylvia, organized a systematic campaign through the Women's Social and Political Union they had founded in 1903. Suffragettes followed a strict strategy: they heckled meetings, rising during an MP's speech, unfurling a banner saying 'Votes for Women' and calling out, 'When will the Liberal Government give the vote to Women?' They were then invariably hustled out, often quite badly knocked about by a combination of hostile police and barracking crowds who would shout 'Why don't you go home to the kitchen stove?'

In 1906 Mrs Pankhurst lobbied the House of Commons; as a result of the skirmish between women and police that ensued, 11 suffragettes went to prison. This was soon to be a familiar pattern, but it did not daunt the women's crusade (see plate 11). Christabel Pankhurst fled to Paris; her mother went on starvation in prison, was released, rearrested, went back on strike. (The 'Cat-and-Mouse Act' had been passed permitting the release of fasting women and allowing for their recapture once they had been restored to health.) From Paris Christabel urged more ferocious measures: windows were smashed by organized

11. In June 1910, 5000 suffragettes, carrying prisoner's arrows marched through London to protest the prison sentence imposed on some of them for their agitation to obtain the right of women to vote.

columns of women with hammers concealed in their handbags; post boxes were set alight; even churches were attacked.

These militants formed only a fringe of the mass movement among women, and they have distracted attention from the huge effort enormous numbers of others made in less spectacular ways to secure their just rights in a society determined to deny them. For the militant campaign for the vote obscured the underlying, more important issue: the desperate need for equal rights that still continues today. In Edwardian Britain women formed half the work force, but at every level earned less than a third or sometimes less than a half of what men earned in the same jobs. Marriage law was weighted against women; a man could sue for divorce on the ground of his wife's adultery, but in a woman's case, his adultery had to be combined with cruelty or desertion. The father had first claim on the children. The view that women were second-class citizens also meant that their special needs were ignored: gynaecology was at a witchdoctor's level of expertise, contraception was associated with prostitution, and therefore difficult of access for the ordinary woman, simple conveniences like disposable sanitary towels had not even been thought of. The suffragette movement was the result of a grievous disequilibrium in the structure of society: it was small wonder it led to such disorder.

The unrest among women was matched by troubles in the male labour force: Edwardian Britain outdid contemporary Britain in strikes. By 1914, only 20 per cent of the work force was organized in unions, and this figure had taken much fighting to achieve. Workers began to realize their contribution was indispensable and undervalued. In 1911 unskilled workers struck in what the historian, Paul Thompson, calls 'almost a mass community protest'; in 1912, 800,000 miners went on strike throughout the nation; that year 40,890,000 working days were lost through strikes. The figure in 1970, one of the worst recent years, was by comparison only 10,980,000.

The prodigal extravagance of the Edwardians was too wasteful of the human lives and sensibilities that fuelled it and serviced it to endure for much longer. It is a remarkable age that finds its workers, women and reactionaries all in revolt against it for their own differing reasons.

In H. G. Wells' novel, *Mr Britling Sees It Through*, written in 1917 about the years before and during the First World War, a Tory lady, who, enraptured with Sir Edward Carson's piratical tactics about Ireland, has taken up the campaign against Home Rule, comes to visit Mr Britling, an eminent writer. Later he comments, and through him, H. G. Wells and many other thinking men of the time are speaking:

> 'The psychology of all this recent insubordination and violence is – curious. Exasperating too. . . . I don't quite grasp it. . . . It's the same thing whether you look at this suffrage business or the labour people

or at this Irish muddle. People may be too safe. You see we live at the end of a series of secure generations in which none of the great things of life have changed materially. We've grown up with no sense of danger – that is to say, with no responsibility. . . . And it's just because we are all convinced that we are so safe against a general breakdown that we are able to be so recklessly violent in our special cases.

'We English are everlasting children in an everlasting nursery. . . .'

But the nursery play was about to come to an end; the destruction to which the England of the 1900s was headed suddenly rushed up at it, as the ground does when a child flings himself down a helter-skelter. The violence at home became as nothing compared to the greater violence on the battlefields of the First World War.

⊠⊠⊠⊠⊠⊠

THE PITY OF WAR

⊠⊠⊠⊠⊠⊠

Here dead we lie because we did not choose
To live and shame the land from which we sprung.
Life, to be sure, is nothing much to lose;
But young men think it is, and we were young.

A. E. HOUSMAN *Here Dead we Lie*

SIEGFRIED SASSOON (see plate 12), poet and soldier in the 2nd Royal Welch Fusiliers, wrote of the battlefields of the First World War: 'I, a single human being, with my little stock of earthly

12. Siegfried Sassoon, painted here by Glyn Philpot, fought in the Battle of the Somme and many others after it, but lived to describe the experience.

experience in my head, was entering once again the veritable gloom and disaster of the thing called Armageddon. And I saw it then, as I see it now – a dreadful place, a place of horror and desolation which no imagination could have invented.' This knowledge became every man's – almost – in the years 1914–18 (see colour plate 1).

The First World War began after Gavrilo Princip, a Serbian student, shot the Archduke Franz Ferdinand, heir to the Austro-Hungarian Empire, and his wife, as they rode past him in an open carriage in the streets of Sarajevo, in the Balkan state of Bosnia. The assassination took place on 28th June, 1914. Austro-Hungary then declared war on Serbia in revenge for the death of the Archduke; Germany supported Austria in her grievance; Russia came in on Serbia's side; Germany, seeing Russia mobilize her armies, mobilized hers and began to march on France, a development that took the German forces through Belgium, a sovereign and neutral country. Great Britain came in to defend Belgium, the great nation protecting the small. This sequence of events, which took the hectic month of July and led to the formal outbreak of war on 4th August, might have been set in motion by anything. It was like a firecracker, jumping across the map of Europe with a series of short, angry explosions. It did not need the assassination of the Archduke; any match might have combusted the highly volatile material of European relations with Germany at that time.

Colonial wars – in South Africa especially, against the Boers – had made peace an important pledge for any government hoping to retain its popularity. Yet, with the Liberals firmly against war, war became the country's choice, the only alternative. The plight of Belgium touched some deep paternal response in the country's collective breast; the English and the French had been dismissing war's possibility yet readying themselves for years; the might of Prussia stirred indignant instincts against the Goliaths who rise up against smaller men; and the variety of ills, social inequality above all, made the cataclysm of war an acceptable, even a welcome, alternative. Yet such explanations only scrape at the surface of the mystery; the springs of human behaviour are hidden so deep in the complexity of human psychology that we will never know why it was, for example, that the British fighting man in the First World War joined up with enthusiasm and fought so bravely and so selflessly in circumstances the horrors of which have never been equalled. Survival was an outside chance.

Yet join up he did, in hundreds of thousands, after the call came from Lord Kitchener, the hero with the handlebar moustache, veteran of many an imperial campaign. 'Your Country Needs You' read the legend under his pointing finger in the recruiting posters.

13. The First World War used mass propaganda to rouse the population's fighting spirit. Posters like this beckoned men to serve, women to man the weapon factories at home.

Lady Cynthia Asquith, daughter-in-law of the Prime Minister, commented after a year of war, when the casualties were already high, 'London, I think, looks distinctly more abnormal now. . . . Raw recruits led by bands still make one cry and everywhere the rather undignified, bullying posters. . . .' (see plate 13). But these posters, and the fervid passionate recruitment, of which these posters were part, tolled the men in: Kitchener's effort had expected to raise one army of 100,000 men, but instead the volunteers flowed in like a torrent. By Spring, 1915, six new armies were formed, each of 100,000 men, all volunteers with no experience of war. Often these men belonged to the same village, or shop, or church. The War Office's organizational resources were soon overwhelmed by this cataract of recruits, so they took it upon themselves to form 'Pals' battalions', in which friends soldiered side by side. Nothing like it had been seen since the fervour of the medieval crusades, when men left families and work to fight the infidel. In 1914, feelings about the 'Hun', or the 'Boches', as the Germans came to be known, resembled closely crusaders' dread of the Saracens as unholy things.

In 1916, compulsory conscription was instituted. The men were not needed. Indeed there were no facilities to train more men, and no equipment to issue them; but warlike feelings in England had reached such a pitch that any able-bodied man, however young or old, who was seen walking the streets at home, was considered a virtual traitor. One of the most blind and cruel customs grew up to brand them cowards: civilians who could not fight – for the most part women – would pin a White Feather on a man's breast to shame him into joining up. So enlistment began. In a way, the people who were left at home were not to blame, for they did not know what it was like to fight: the Press was censored, not a single journalist was present in the battles, the Government refused to give any information at all, partly because the news was usually bad, partly because they did not know what to say, for they did not know themselves what was happening. But the huge appetite for war that consumed those who did not have to fight was an ugly phenomenon, because compassion had no place in it.

It was the men who fought in the trenches who felt the pity.

14. The experience of the trenches provided an extraordinary stimulus to poetry. A new, brilliant, hard, painful imagery was born, most notably from the genius of Wilfred Owen, photographed here on leave with his nephew.

Wilfred Owen (see plate 14), one of this century's finest poets, expressed it in his great poem 'Strange Meeting'. He has a vision that he escapes the fighting and finds himself, like Dante, in the infernal regions, where the dead lie all about. But one man springs up and speaks to him of war, of how men must be warned about its wickedness and its waste. He mourns 'the undone years, the hopelessness'.
He tells him the truth must be told:

> 'The pity of war, the pity war distilled.
> Now men will go content with what we spoiled.
> Or, discontent, boil bloody and be spilled.'

Then he reveals himself to the poet:

> 'I am the enemy you killed, my friend.
> I knew you in this dark; for so you frowned
> Yesterday through me as you jabbed and killed.
> I parried; but my hands were loath and cold.
> Let us sleep now. . . .'

So the poem ends, underlining the fellowship of all men in pain and death, however bitterly they might be made to stand up against each other by the tragic conjunctions of politics.

Wilfred Owen was killed one week before the Armistice in 1918. He was leading his company of men across a canal, showing the astonishing bravery characteristic of so many soldiers in that war. He had fought one long stint on the Somme river earlier in the war, and then been hospitalized in England for shell shock, the name given to the breakdown many suffered after exposure to Armageddon. It was typical that men who were broken down in this way, or wounded, were quickly patched up and sent out again to fight, or, as in Wilfred Owen's case, to die. What many men longed for was a 'Blighty' wound – one that would get them sent home for good, but not disable them completely.

What was Armageddon, the fighting line, like? At first the Germans had planned to swing down through Belgium and encircle the French, taking Paris. Their armies would be on the move, as in earlier wars. But the First World War established a new kind of battle, in which there was no movement: trench warfare. The advance on Paris was halted by the British, and the Germans began to retreat, pursued by the British. The historian, A. J. P. Taylor, has described what happened then: 'the weary Germans, unable to march further, stopped on the Aisne. Unwittingly, they stumbled on the discovery which shaped the First World War: men in trenches with machine guns could beat off all but the most formidable attacks.'

By the end of 1914, only a few months after the beginning of the war, a continuous line of trenches stretched across north-east France from the German frontier near Verdun to the sea north of Ypres. At this stage the lines were not very deep; but by mid-1916 trenches formed a huge, labyrinthine network from the front line stretching back deep to an organization of military bases, hospitals, supply depots, offices and relief areas.

The front line of the Germans was sometimes only 40 yards from the British or French front line: the soldiers could hear each other talking. The ground in between was called No Man's Land; it was the scene of the fiercest fighting, for an advance in the First World War was measured in yards, not miles. To the Welsh poet and artist, David Jones, No Man's Land was a lunar landscape, and he describes its shattered and cratered surface in his prose poem, *In Parenthesis*:

> Slime-glisten on the churnings up, fractured earth pilings, heaped on, heaped up waste; overturned far throwings; tottering perpendiculars lean and sway; more leper-trees pitted, rownsepyked out of nature, cut off in their sap-rising.
>
> Saturate, littered, rusted coilings, metallic rustlings, thin ribboned-metal chafing – rasp low for some tension freed; by rat, or wind disturbed. Smooth-rippled discs gleamed, where gaping craters, their brimming waters, made mirror for the sky procession – bear up before the moon incongruous souvenirs. Margarine tins sail derelict, where little eddies quivered, wind caught, their sharp-jagged twisted lids wrenched back.

This was the only sight of the world the soldiers in the trenches saw. Otherwise they lived underground, in these long corridors of impacted earth, built with a parapet facing the enemy, and redoubts for machine gun emplacements (see plate 15). The trenches formed a continuous line, with communication ditches running into them at right angles from the rear; they were built with a series of kinks in them called traverses, so that an enemy jumping down into one could not shoot the whole length of a single trench. This also meant that each company of men was alone in its section of the earthworks. Along the trenches ran 'the wires', the only method by which the staff headquarters could keep in touch with the officers; but once the men 'went over the top', that is, leaving the trenches, moved into the attack, they also left the telephone behind them and were out of touch with

15. Wyndham Lewis was one of the great originals in the exciting prewar art movement which he named 'Vorticism'. He tried, as in this painting, *A Battery Shelled*, to capture the essence of the machine age's dynamic forms.

command. The trenches' floors were lined with duckboards, but as they continually filled with water, the duckboards floated about, creating another hazard. There were rats; there were lice which devoured men so badly they caught 'Trench Fever' from the bites. Isaac Rosenberg, who was killed in the fighting on the Western Front in April, 1918, was a painter, and a poet of considerable tortured power and vivid, even grotesque imagination. With his sense of the monstrous, he described the men looking for lice:

> Then we all sprang up and stripped
> To hunt the verminous brood. . . .
> See gargantuan hooked fingers
> Pluck in supreme flesh
> To smutch supreme littleness.

The quarters smelt of disinfectant, when they did not smell of something worse; there were only dugouts to sleep in and they afforded little shelter against the cold which was often severe.

4. *Communicating with Prisoners*, showing Nationalist fighters talking to their wives below the jail, was painted by Jack Yeats in 1924, when the acute troubles in Ireland moved this essentially private painter to treat public issues.

5. T. S. Eliot, a pessimistic poet with an exceptional gift for imagery, was painted in 1938 by Percy Wyndham Lewis, himself a writer and a painter of forceful originality.

6. William Roberts, an early Vorticist who has continued to develop his unique style of English Cubism, painted *The Cinema* in 1965, recalling the days when films provided the most popular entertainment.

Wilfred Owen described the horror of January, 1917, in a letter to his mother. His platoon

> had to lie in the snow under the deadly wind. By day it was impossible to stand up or even crawl about because we were behind only a little ridge screening us from the Boches' periscope.
>
> We had 5 Tommy's cookers between the Platoon, but they did not suffice to melt the ice in the water-cans. So we suffered cruelly from thirst.
>
> The marvel is that we did not all die of cold. As a matter of fact, only one of my party actually froze to death before he could be got back. . . .
>
> I was kept warm by the ardour of Life within me. I forgot hunger in the hunger for Life. The intensity of your Love reached me and kept me living. . . .

Badly equipped, poorly trained, maltreated by conditions like these and often given impossible instructions by men who had never even seen the lie of the land, this volunteer army outdid itself in courage when it came to battle. The Battle of the Somme was the name given to the enormous push made by the British and French against the German line; it started on 1st July, 1916, along an immensely long front; it continued through till November. The plan of attack sounded splendid. A barrage of artillery fire would thunder full blast against the German lines, then lift, then come down again in full fury deeper in their midst. The idea was that the infantry soldiers would follow behind the artillery barrage, arriving just as it lifted in ground presumably flattened and freed from all enemy defenders.

For three days before zero hour, 21,000 tons of shells were hurled by 50,000 gunners into the German territory the British planned to gain. The noise was infernal, ear-splitting, head-splitting, enough to concuss all the soldiers before the fighting even began; and it was almost all in vain. When the British divisions left their trenches at zero hour on 1st July, their appearance in No Man's Land was greeted by salvoes of machine-gun fire from the Germans. The bombardment had battered helplessly on the earth fortifications above the dug-in Germans, and their

16. At the Battle of the Somme, English soldiers were picked off by enemy fire as they tried to struggle through their own defensive wire outside the trenches. William Roberts, in this 1972 drawing, *On the Wire*, recalled the tragedy.

guns were still mostly in place. Very little high explosive had been used in the shells, and it was high explosive alone that could destroy the German positions. Nor could the attacking English move quickly, for they carried enormous amounts of equipment in packs on their backs, including masks to protect them from the poison gas the Germans began using in April, 1915. Worse, the bombardment had not even cut the huge bales of barbed wire defending trench positions, so that the attackers found themselves hunting for gaps under the full eye of the enemy. William Roberts, then a War Artist commissioned by the government, painted the terrible sight of soldiers hanging dead from the wire where they were caught, snagged like so much torn clothing (see plate 16).

Wave after wave of soldiers attacked in the Battle of the Somme, as the plan ordered them to; wave after wave came down. Losing communication with their high command, they also lost touch with the artillery barrage which advanced according to the strategy, and could not be recalled, though the soldiers had stopped following under its protection, because they were either dead, or struggling in hand-to-hand combat.

This was the character of battle in the First World War; it was called the 'war of attrition', because each side sought to win by wearing down the other's manpower; soldier was to kill soldier until, by process of elimination, the victor would be left alone in the field, empty but for the dead. By this standard, the British suffered a terrible defeat in the Battle of the Somme. There were about 60,000 British casualties, 21,000 were dead, most of them killed in the first hour, if not the first few moments of the fight. In the First World War overall, there were three officers killed for every private, for the officers led their men and often took the brunt of the first fire. Many of these company commanders were schoolboys, and completely inexperienced. One private remembered his platoon being asked who amongst them had bowled well at cricket, for the skill might help in throwing hand grenades. There was a special medal instituted to reward young officers for conspicuous gallantry: the Military Cross. Wilfred Owen was awarded it, posthumously. Sassoon's bravery won him the MC just before the Battle of the Somme, as well as the war nickname 'Mad Jack'. With colloquial, curt irony, he expressed the bungling, the crassness and the cruelty of the war in the trenches. In

one of his celebrated poems he describes the harsh scene after a
battle – it may have been the Somme:

> The place was rotten with dead; green clumsy legs
> High booted, sprawled and grovelled along the saps
> And trunks, face downward, in the sucking mud,
> Wallowed like trodden sand-bags loosely filled;
> And naked sodden buttocks, mats of hair,
> Bulged, clotted heads slept in the plastering slime.
> And then the rain began, – the jolly old rain!

When the war ended, one in every ten Edwardian men under 45
had been killed; one in five wounded. Yet the emotions of men
enduring this holocaust were often surprisingly mild. When we
hear their voices, in the songs and the poems and the diaries of
the war, they can rise with strong, ironical cheerfulness.

Siegfried Sassoon, with his particularly cool brand of burning
pity, caught the tolerance, and the innocence of the men in many
of his poems. 'The General' is rightly famous:

> 'Good-morning; good-morning!' the General said
> When we met him last week on our way to the line.
> Now the soldiers he smiled at are most of 'em dead,
> And we're cursing his staff for incompetent swine.
> 'He's a cheery ole card', grunted Harry to Jack
> As they slogged up to Arras with rifle and pack.
>
> But he did for them both by his plan of attack.

The songs of the First World War, written mostly by anony-
mous soldiers to the tunes of Victorian hymns or music hall turns,
are unique: the Second World War produced nothing like them.
They are sarcastic and bitter, but the melancholy is cut across
with a stout-hearted jollity. They laugh at themselves, at their
incompetence, at their predicament:

> Why did we join the army, boys?
> Why did we join the army?
> Why did we come to France to fight?
> We must have been bloody well barmy.

Sometimes the knowledge that they could never make people at home understand or share their experience, comes through with irony:

> And when they ask us how dangerous it was
> Oh! we'll never tell them,
> Oh we'll never tell them.
> We spent our pay in some café. . . .
> It was the cushiest job we ever had. . . .

The officers, especially in the first two years of the war, were exhilarated by the fight. It is a curious thing, and a deeply disturbing aspect of human psychology, but men enjoy war. The First World War inspired daring and self-sacrifice to a remarkable degree. Julian Grenfell, one of the gifted, golden youths who joined up in 1914 soon found the death he seemed almost to woo. In his poem 'Into Battle', he had exulted in the idea of dying:

> And he is dead who will not fight;
> And who dies fighting has increase.

Sassoon himself, the most powerful anti-war voice, is powerful precisely because he understood the seductiveness of war. He wondered in the diary he wrote at the time about 'that sense of immolation to some vague aspiration . . . self-sacrifice, emotion at facing danger unafraid, and that queer hankering for extinction which I can't explain.'

The poems of the officers and the songs of the men celebrate that other aspect of war that thrills men who fight: the feeling of comradeship, of union with your fellow men. Wilfred Owen, when another great poet, Robert Graves, remonstrated against the unmitigated bleakness of his poetry, wrote a new poem to commemorate the friendship and the glory in the front line:

> Faces that used to curse me, scowl for scowl,
> Shine and lift up with passion of oblation,
> Seraphic for an hour; though they were foul.

Robert Graves, poet, classicist, historian, and one of the most original men alive, himself wrote a vivid account of fighting in the

First World War, his autobiography, *Goodbye To All That* (1929). He does not share Sassoon's hard edge, but he does celebrate the same qualities of courage and endurance and comradeship. His book is a discursive, lively, attractive portrait of himself as a young man after 'a conditioning in the Protestant morality of the English governing classes, though qualified by mixed blood, a rebellious nature, and an overriding poetic obsession.' He is a marvellous story-teller and companion, and the account of the horrors of the trenches is softened throughout by throwaway wit and generous humanity. In an account of the battle during which he was wounded, Graves is capable of telling a story of official incompetence:

> Division could always be trusted to send a warning about verdigris on vermorel-sprayers, or the keeping of pets in trenches, or being polite to our allies, or some other triviality, exactly when an attack was in progress. This time orders came for a private in 'C' company to report immediately . . . The private was charged with the murder of a French civilian in an estaminet at Béthune a month previously. It seems that a good deal of cognac had been going round, and the French civilian, who bore a grudge against the British because of his faithless wife, began to insult the private. He was reported, somewhat improbably, as having said: 'Anglais no bon, Allmand très bon. War fineesh, napoo les Anglais. Allmand win.' The private had thereupon drawn his bayonet and run the man through. At the court martial the private was exonerated; the French civil representative commending him for having 'energetically repressed local defeatism.'
> The soldier and his escort missed the battle.

The war stirred men's imaginations to an intense degree. Owen was passionately against it; yet he rejoined the fighting with enthusiasm. Sassoon, a gallant and generous soul, was so horrified by the progress of the war and the useless sacrifice of thousands of lives that, in July, 1917, while home on leave, he threw his medal into the river Mersey, and issued a statement that exploded on the English at home like the shells they knew nothing about. Sassoon simply demanded to know the aims of the war.

It seems extraordinary now, but few people knew why the war continued to be fought. At first Belgium had been the issue; but no one had formally asked the Germans to leave Belgium, and the war would certainly not have stopped if they had left. The nations became like prize-fighters, so punch-drunk with beating each other about the head that they no longer knew how to stop. Also, other battle areas had opened up – in Gallipoli in Turkey, in Mesopotamia to defend British access to Persian oil wells, in Palestine (Jerusalem fell to the British at the end of 1917). To thoughtful men, the war no longer seemed 'a war of defence and liberation', but 'a war of aggression and conquest'. Sassoon spoke for a few people who, sickened by the death toll, wanted peace by negotiation, not total victory. But the Government wanted to crush German might for ever – though Lloyd George, the most talented member committed to the war, expressed it differently – and so the war wore on.

The soldiers did not feel the intense hatred of 'the Hun' that civilians felt. Instead, they often expressed a fatalistic belief that all soldiers, on both sides, were part of some grand, inexorable design which fated them to fight and die. Isaac Rosenberg, a most reluctant soldier, saw God as a malign presence seeking to destroy the world, and dreamed of somehow cheating him of his spoils: 'by pretending to have as much misery as we can bear, so that it (our malignant fate) withholds its greater evil, while under that guise of misery there is secret joy. . . .' In 1917, Lady Cynthia Asquith expressed the same idea in other terms: 'Would it be easier if one hated the Germans? I feel them – poor devils – to be our wretched allies fighting against some third thing. The whole thing *must* be the means to some end, and that no political one.'

Her doubts were becoming more common, but the gung-ho oratory of the warmongers still kept the country anxious for total victory over the Germans. Ironically, it was feared that any negotiated settlement would lead to a resurgence of German power later. In practice, defeat led to the same result.

The war did come to an end – by military means, and more swiftly than the military men expected. The Americans, led by the pacifist President, Woodrow Wilson, had refrained from joining in, but in April, 1917, the more belligerent prevailed, and the US army arrived to fight in Europe for the first time. Their troops helped towards the ultimate victory. The Germans launched an offensive on the Western Front in July, 1918, and it failed. From then on the stalemate began to yield; in Turkey, in Syria, the British began to break through the Germans' defences. In October, the German Government, fearing outright defeat, appealed to President Wilson to open peace negotiations. On 11th November, Germany signed the Armistice, and Europe was at peace again.

The 'Fourteen Points', as the agreement Wilson drew up was called, guaranteed amongst other things the independence of small nations. It set up the League of Nations to try and ensure this. It readjusted national boundaries where Germany had absorbed them, giving back independence to Poland and Serbia and Bulgaria. Mr Britling, Wells' character, expressed the widespread idealism about each nation's sovereignty that it was hoped the War would bring: The First World War would lead to an 'end to the folly and vanity of kings, and to any people ruling any people but themselves. There is no convenience, there is no justice, in any people ruling any people but themselves; the ruling of men by others, who have not their creeds and their languages and their ignorances and prejudices, that is the fundamental folly. . . .'

His idea is utopian; Wilson's Fourteen Points could no more create such harmony of self-determination in the map of the world than they could bring down the moon. German defeat would rankle for two decades, only to erupt again, in the Second World War.

The First, meanwhile, had wiped out 947,000 men of the British Empire, and left another million and a half disabled by wounds or gas. But this is chicken-feed compared to the French and Russian cannon fodder: 1,400,000 French dead, 1,700,000 Russian. As for the enemy, they had suffered even more terrible casualties: 1,800,000 Germans had died; 1,200,000 Austro-Hungarians. Taking in the other countries who had been involved, the toll added to over $8\frac{1}{2}$ million.

Death was the greatest visible consequence of the war; but what it meant, how it affected England can never be seized by a set of figures. England was a changed nation afterwards. In politics, culture, morals, attitudes and expectations, she had undergone a revolution. It was a revolution that began with the fissures in Edwardian society, and widened them in order to render that society obsolete.

ROCKS OF REAL LIFE

> Remember us – if at all – not as lost
> Violent souls, but only
> As the hollow men
> The stuffed men.
>
> T. S. ELIOT *The Hollow Men*

A NEW world would be created: immediately after the war, this was not just a hope against hope, it seemed to most people a certainty. 1919 began in a mood of euphoria. Everything was possible. Sassoon burst out with his most famous rapturous poem:

> Everyone suddenly burst out singing;
> And I was filled with such delight
> As prisoned birds must find in freedom,
> Winging wildly across the white
> Orchards and dark-green fields; on-on-and out of sight.
>
> Everyone's voice was suddenly lifted;
> And beauty came like the setting sun:
> My heart was shaken with tears; and horror
> Drifted away . . . O, but Everyone
> Was a bird; and the song was wordless; the singing will never be done.

On another spoke of the social wheel, the revolutionary Rosa Luxemburg expressed a similar optimism: 'We shall still live and experience great things. What we are witnessing first of all is the whole old world sinking, each day a piece, a new collapse, a fresh gigantic overthrow. . . .' Lloyd George (see plate 17), Prime

17. Jacob Epstein's sculpture is marked by elemental energy and love of massive forms. His bust of Lloyd George, above, catches the leader's powerful vitality.

Minister of the Coalition Government that, uniting Unionists (Conservatives) and Liberals had run the country since 1916, called an election in 1918 and brought about a personal triumph. He was the 'Man Who Won the War': he was going to fulfil his promise to make a country 'fit for heroes' to live in. The voters gave him a large majority, for they believed his new government could rebuild England.

Lloyd George is the single gigantic figure, apart from Churchill, amongst the Prime Ministers of this century. A solicitor from a poverty-stricken rural district of Wales, he was brilliant, eloquent, passionate, hard-driving, irrepressible. Short and slightly built, with a lion's head of white hair and a penetrating glance, he relied on his innate cunning and wiliness to get by. When facing a crisis he would lie in bed reading thrillers, or go on a long walk in the country, trusting to his gift of improvisation to make the right decision. He operated through family, lifelong friends, and dubious business contacts, rather than through the party machinery or even Parliament, saying of himself: 'I never believed in costly frontal attacks, either in war or politics, if there were a way round.' He was a radical champion of the poor by temperament who, in 1909, as Chancellor of the Exchequer, introduced a rise in income tax on the rich so that the State could afford protections for the poor. Thus, he initiated the theme that has dominated twentieth century politics in Britain: the responsibility of the State towards all its citizens. Lloyd George's 'People's Budget' of 1909 provoked a storm then; but its central tenet, that the fat of the land must be made to go round, prevailed against a mighty opposition of vested interests. The seed of the idea, that the economy should be managed by the Government in order to distribute wealth with greater justice throughout the community, was sown before the war; it greatly flourished during the war when, for instance, food supplies had to be controlled by the Government and rationing made no difference between rich and poor; it seemed the revolutionary force that would wipe out the old Edwardian inequalities.

In some ways the world was turned upside down. But the process was more sluggish than the immediate post-war euphoria had surmised, and much less dazzling than Lloyd George's righteous anger had promised.

The areas that had provoked crisis after crisis before and during the War were suddenly becalmed. In 1918, unobtrusively, without fuss or opposition, women over 30 got the vote. It was extended to all adults, including women over 21, in 1928. The principle, so long fought over, was conceded quietly. The suffragettes had attracted attention to the injustice by their violent methods; the huge, moderate mass of ordinary women who had contributed to the war effort by working in the factories and on the land while the soldiers fought at the Front knew they had earned equality with men (see plate 18).

Feminists became free to address the greater problem, of women's inequality in history. Virginia Woolf (see colour plate 2), an extraordinary novelist of sensibility and subtlety, published

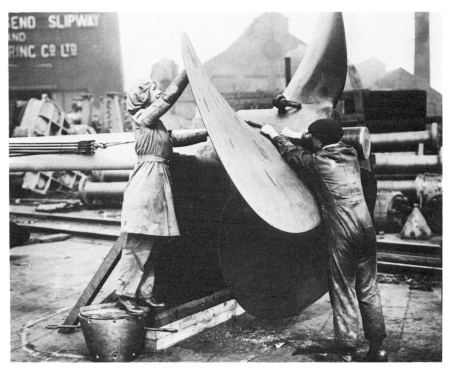

18. Women making propellers during the First World War. Their enormous contribution to the war effort helped to quell prejudice against them afterwards.

one of her most brilliant essays, *A Room of One's Own*, in 1928, in which she discussed, with a combination of drollery and seriousness, the reason why there has never been a female Shakespeare. She rooted this in women's oppression by social convention and psychological expectation: her argument, that culture has compounded women's inferiority over the ages, is still the fundamental basis of feminist discussion of the problem. Virginia Woolf describes what would have been the fate of Shakespeare's sister, if he had had one:

> Meanwhile his extraordinarily gifted sister, let us suppose, remained at home. She was as adventurous, as imaginative, as agog to see the world as he was. But she was not sent to school. She had no chance of learning grammar and logic, let alone reading Horace and Virgil. She picked up a book now and then, one of her brother's

perhaps, and read a few pages. But then her parents came in and told her to mend the stockings or mind the stew and not moon about with books and papers. They would have spoken sharply but kindly, for they were substantial people who knew the conditions of life for a woman and loved their daughter. . . .

Women had got the vote, but it did not resolve their problems; Ireland got Home Rule, but the Irish question troubles England still. In 1921, under Lloyd George's premiership, Ireland was partitioned, with the six counties of the North remaining under British rule with their own parliament, and the twenty-six counties of the South becoming the Irish Free State, at this stage a dominion. (But it later achieved independence by constitutional means.) This development appeared then a brilliant solution to the bitter conflicts; but it has proved a temporary answer.

Great steps were made to improve the lot of the working class: the Unemployment Insurance Act of 1920 extended the 'dole' to all people out of work (in 1911 the industries of engineering, building and shipbuilding only had won this protection from the State). The year before, the Housing and Town Planning Act set aside the first government funds to build houses. Such acts were fundamental in shaping the relationship between the State and the individual that is today considered commonplace and normal.

But in the vital areas of education and industrial relations, very little indeed was done. In order to survive, Lloyd George could not act upon advice he himself sought when it proved too radical for the politicians who kept him in power. For instance, the Sankey Commission in 1919 recommended that miners should be better paid and work shorter hours. Conditions in the mines were a national scandal: the great novelist of the Twenties, D. H. Lawrence, one of the few English literary geniuses to come from a working-class background, described the harshness and poverty of a miner's life in his autobiographical masterpiece, *Sons and Lovers*. The Sankey Commission, trying to remedy the situation, even proposed state control of the industry. But Lloyd George failed to take up these proposals, and his failure is one of the many disastrous stations on the long via dolorosa in the history of miners' grievances that is still causing trouble today.

Lloyd George cannot be held altogether responsible for this kind of failure: inaction was endemic in the inter-war period amongst all political men and parties. Fear of such a revolution as took place in Russia in 1917, overturning an ancient despotic regime and abolishing all private property, terrorized Western Europe: the word 'terror' is too mild. Even Socialists within the Labour party were meekened by the spectacle of communism triumphant.

The next Prime Minister, the Conservative Bonar Law, was suffering from cancer of the throat; he resigned, and Stanley Baldwin became Prime Minister in his stead. Bonar Law's motto had been 'Tranquillity'; Baldwin's was to be 'Safety First'. With the exception of the important nine months from 1924 to 1925 when the first Labour Government took office and then lost it, the Conservatives under Baldwin were in power until virtually the end of the decade. They cast a lustreless look over the entire political history of the times.

The most conspicuous achievement of the first Labour Government was that it held office at all: it proved that the Labour Party, which had only been formed in 1906, and which contained only one politician with firsthand experience of government – Arthur Henderson who had served in the Coalition cabinet during the war – was capable of running the country. This, in the England of the 1920's, with its tepidity and traditionalism, was a major success.

The ideas upon which the Labour movement had been built were expressed by the thinkers and reformers in the Fabian Society, an association dedicated – in a paternalist and utilitarian way – to redressing the disadvantages and inequalities of the working class. Men and women like Sidney and Beatrice Webb, the philosopher and historian R. H. Tawney, the playwright George Bernard Shaw all contributed to drawing up a scheme of moral and social reform that would benefit the workers of the country. George Bernard Shaw reached a wide audience, through his wise-cracking wit which delighted in dizzy sequences of paradoxes to expose the prejudices and assumptions of the English upper classes. In *Man and Superman*, for instance, the hero's chauffeur is bright as a new pin, and shows up the silliness of his masters. He is one of the new men, educated sensibly at a polytechnic. His employers have been to Oxbridge, where he says scornfully, they have learned to be gentlemen, but not much else.

The first Labour Government did not succeed in putting into practice many of the Fabian theories of social equality – it fell too soon. A scandal erupted over a letter from the Russian president of the Communist International, Zinoviev, exhorting the British to revolution through the Labour Party. The letter was probably forged, but the reaction shows how inflammable fears were about reds under the bed.

The return of England to Tory guidance in 1925 did not stop the drift towards collectivism: the state took on more and more of the responsibility for the welfare of its members. In education, public health, pensions, roads and other public services, many reforms were introduced which cast the safety net against destitution wider than ever before. But they were makeshift, piecemeal improvements, and the roots of inequality were not really touched.

The even tenor of the Baldwin premiership was interrupted by an event that can be seen now as entirely tragic. It was the major political upheaval of the inter-war years. From 3rd May, 1926, for nine days, there was a strike of all workers in essential services. Food was distributed by the Army; a few volunteers (see plate 19), most of them upper-class students who did not know what they were doing, provided transport; but the country was at a standstill for a time, resembling the 'Sleeping Beauty' castle when, by enchantment, everyone has been put to sleep. Except that this was very desperate: the General Strike was a cataclysm. Both sides had placed themselves in such a position that one or other must be either the victor or the loser. There could be, after a General Strike, no half-measures: in this extremism lay the tragedy.

It happened because the mines were losing money, and all proposals for the regeneration of the industry had been left on paper in a Whitehall drawer. The owners, unregenerate and blind,

THE SPIRIT OF ENGLAND AT WORK: RAILWAY AND DOCK VOLUNTEERS.

PHOTOGRAPHS BY SPORT AND GENERAL, TOPICAL, I.N.A., AND KEYSTONE.

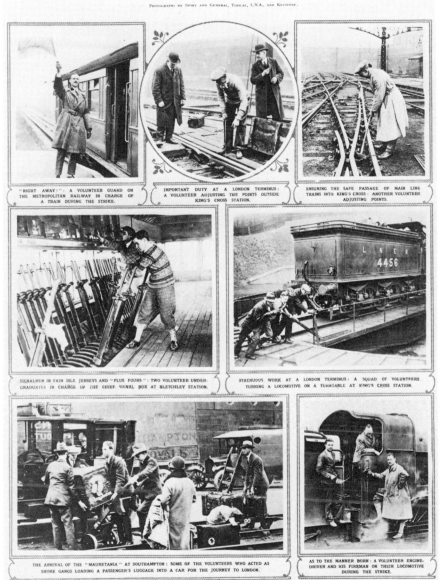

"RIGHT AWAY!": A VOLUNTEER GUARD ON THE METROPOLITAN RAILWAY IN CHARGE OF A TRAIN DURING THE STRIKE.

IMPORTANT DUTY AT A LONDON TERMINUS: A VOLUNTEER ADJUSTING THE POINTS OUTSIDE KING'S CROSS STATION.

ENSURING THE SAFE PASSAGE OF MAIN LINE TRAINS INTO KING'S CROSS: ANOTHER VOLUNTEER ADJUSTING POINTS.

SIGNALMEN IN FAIR ISLE JERSEYS AND "PLUS FOURS": TWO VOLUNTEER UNDER-GRADUATES IN CHARGE OF THE CHIEF SIGNAL BOX AT BLETCHLEY STATION.

STRENUOUS WORK AT A LONDON TERMINUS: A SQUAD OF VOLUNTEERS TURNING A LOCOMOTIVE ON A TURNTABLE AT KING'S CROSS STATION.

THE ARRIVAL OF THE "MAURETANIA" AT SOUTHAMPTON: SOME OF THE VOLUNTEERS WHO ACTED AS SHORE GANGS LOADING A PASSENGER'S LUGGAGE INTO A CAR FOR THE JOURNEY TO LONDON.

AS TO THE MANNER BORN: A VOLUNTEER ENGINE-DRIVER AND HIS FIREMAN ON THEIR LOCOMOTIVE DURING THE STRIKE.

19. May, 1926: the only time all Britain's workers went on general strike. The essential services, like the buses and trains, were continued by volunteers who for the most part did not understand the meaning of strike-breaking.

suggested that in order to improve profits, the men should work longer hours for less money. It seems almost inconceivable today that such a notion would even be considered, let alone voiced. The miners rebelled. Their slogan was: 'Not a penny off the pay, not a minute on the day'.

Intransigence, mainly on the owners' side, drove the miners into a deeper state of rebellion. After months in which each side met the other with prevarications, demands, and further prevarications, the belligerent wing of the cabinet – including Churchill – prevailed against Baldwin's anxious and moderate stand, and forced a showdown. The miners were locked out from their places of work; a General Strike was called by the Trades Union Congress to support their fellows, and all British workers struck to express their sympathy.

Nine days later, the Government would still not yield to the miners' demands. Nowadays these seem so mild and so reasonable, that it can hardly be believed that Churchill and his sympathizers were raging furiously against them and demanding 'unconditional surrender'. The Trades Union leaders, afraid for the terrible consequences of a prolonged period of no work, no money, no resources for the working man, gave in as the Government wanted them to do, thus betraying the cause they had adopted. But they really had no alternative.

This complete humiliation of the working man in his greatest bid to redress the imbalance of the old society, in his moment of greatest risk-taking, was seen then by the ruling class as total triumph, but the ugly and cruel defeat of the General Strike has left a legacy of bitterness between workers and bosses that is with us still. The erosion of class conflict that to some extent was achieved by the shared experience of the war and its hardship, and by the dismantling of a certain kind of country-style high living after the war was forgotten when the interests of employers were glorified by a short-term victory.

The historian, Charles Loch Mowat, wrote: 'It was afterwards said that the strike was defeated by the community; by the ordinary people rallying to support the Government. In such a context "ordinary people" means the middle classes.' Another writer commented: '. . . the strike only showed what was known already, that people who dress like gentlemen will instinctively take sides against people who commonly work with their coats off . . .'

In 1929, the people who worked with their coats off threw out the Tories and elected the second Labour Government, again under the leadership of Ramsay MacDonald. This time Labour could again achieve very little, not just because they were once more in a minority position, but also because a worldwide financial crisis, the 'Crash' of 1929, hit England, causing terrible unemployment and near bankruptcy of the pound. Unbelievably, the only solution was thought to be a cut in the unemployment benefits paid to men out of work. Ramsay MacDonald responded to the crisis by asking for the resignation of his own Labour cabinet, in favour of a National Government which he would lead. For the second time in five years the Labour movement was betrayed; but this time, the kiss was bestowed by its own leader. It turned out that Ramsay MacDonald, a handsome, fluent man of signal bonhomie, loved to survive and lead above all principles. Thus he became a Prime Minister in what was really a Conservative Government, and he decided that the men who were out of work through no fault of their own should suffer. Lloyd George railed helplessly: 'This ranting hero of the Socialist halls squealed with terror when he was invited to face the wrath of the financial weasels of the City. What leaders for a Revolution!'

In 1931 very few people had grasped the economic principle that now seems very simple to us: that if you want to sell goods you must have goods to sell, that if you ask people to make goods and pay them to do it then they will have money to buy other goods. In 1931, the Government, faced with a shop that was losing money, decided the best way to slow down the losses was not to buy any more stock. That way, they were well on to the road to bare shelves for everyone and no customers at all.

The National Government of 1931 inaugurated the era of the Thirties, during which the hopes of a new world that had been entertained after the War became at best a dimly remembered dream. Opportunities to reconstruct, opportunities for change, so many had been lost. And why?

One of the reasons remains endemic in British society. Politics did not attract; the war left a generation deeply disillusioned with all forms of public life, inured to the fascination of leadership, dead to the idea of social responsibility. For however humdrum the Twenties was in official life, it was a brilliant decade in the arts, in letters, in the development of private philosophies of life, and even, on a less lofty plane, in the pursuit of fun. But the issues and tragedies of the day find very little mention in the masterpieces of the age. With the exception of Lawrence, who sprang from poverty, the writers of the times were privileged, and even when their consciences were active they remained distant from the tussles of unemployment and hardship. They battled in the arena of ideas – an important arena, where work with lasting effect is undertaken. But they were not concerned with the immediate problems of society.

It is significant that there is really only one major figure of the decade who spans the divide between the world of public affairs and the world of private letters. John Maynard Keynes (see plate 20) was the economist and political philosopher who demonstrated the axioms by which English financial policy has been conducted since the Second World War. Lloyd George consulted Keynes early on, and in his manifesto for the 1929 campaign 'We Can Conquer Unemployment' he had outlined Keynes' expansionist theories about job creation and wealth creation that have since become accepted ideas. But Keynes was not only a boffin: he moved in the social and intellectual circle that has become known as 'Bloomsbury'.

'Bloomsbury' was a social phenomenon, an extended family of writers, artists, thinkers who were individually gifted to varying degrees but yet, as a group, generated high voltage imagination and creativity. Their work has attracted less attention recently than the intricate knitting patterns of their sex lives; but the question who slept with whom in Bloomsbury is really only of interest because it reveals one important aspect of their collective

20. The economic theories of John Maynard Keynes are still central to Labour Party thinking. Here he is drawn by Gwen Raverat, a friend who was also linked to the Bloomsbury group through a Cambridge background.

character: that they were unconventional and desirous of flouting tradition, even down to their love affairs. Bloomsbury was a crucial step in a sad process, because it finally established a literary sensibility that could not be popular; it developed a canon of aesthetics that excluded the general reader, or viewer, or sampler. It was exclusive; it personified the age in which we still live, with an avant-garde culture, considered incomprehensible by most people, opposed to a popular culture, which intellectuals often think beneath them. Though the tradition of this clash is very ancient, there had been, in the era before the Twenties, many figures who appeared to ignore it altogether and thus to make it vanish: George Bernard Shaw, whose popular plays bristled with epigrams, witticisms, socialist arguments, sophistries and fun; Arnold Bennett, once editor of *Woman* magazine, best-selling novelist, spokesman for taste before and during the War; and H. G. Wells, scientist, novelist and historian of distinction.

But the members of Bloomsbury never caught the ear of the ordinary man. Though they professed socialist ideas, and, for instance, in the Omega art workshops tried to revive traditional British standards of craftsmanship, they practised a rarefied art, deeply expressive of the fragmentation that had occurred in society. It is an art that made it impossible any longer for one man to talk to everyone in a common tongue.

The trenches had killed the burgeoning pre-war avant-garde: Gaudier-Brzeska (see plate 21), holding the promise to be one of the greatest sculptors of our time, died fighting for the French in 1918. Vorticism, the movement to which he had contributed, was formed and led by the writer and painter, Wyndham Lewis, a brilliant, erratic and dogmatic man. But Vorticism, called after the

21. Influenced by African art, Henri Gaudier-Brzeska was so bold and adventurous that his work, like this *Bird Swallowing a Fish*, influenced modern sculpture long after his death in 1918.

Vortex of dynamic movement which the painters sought to capture in their work, was shattered by the war. The few members who survived 1914–18 pursued their own art independently afterwards, like the master of form, William Roberts, who is still alive, and the poet of sparkling, bizarre images, Edith Sitwell.

Bloomsbury was different, it was a force in literary and artistic society. Virginia Woolf (see colour plate 2) was its only genius – if one discounts Keynes' more practical spirit. A novelist of immense stature, capable of portraying the inner landscape of a man or woman's mind, she is totally absorbed in the eternally fascinating problem of human character. She approaches the people in her books through the small domestic details surrounding them in their ordinary lives, and then moves through this circumstantial frame to the spirit within to create lasting effects of harmony and order. Thus in *Mrs Dalloway* (1925), Woolf's edgy mannered style picks up the subtle ebb and flow of emotion between people; in *The Waves* (1931), the characters speak of each other in different voices, each separately registering turmoil, conflict, joy. The ultra-sensitive fluidity of her prose in the novels might lead one to imagine that she herself had no substance, that she was perhaps tiresome and a little fey. So it is reassuring to find how robust, how tart, how funny, sharp-eyed and spirited she is in her essays and her criticism.

It was probably the magnetism of Virginia Woolf's exceptional gifts that kept the Bloomsbury circle an entity. Lady Ottoline Morrell, a larger-than-life patroness of numerous artists and a committed pacifist, caught in her diary the lofty heights Virginia Woolf occupied and the powerful, almost trance-like effect she could have on people:

> I thought her extraordinarily beautiful and supremely eminent. Her generalizations and her swiftness of mind astounded me. She sat as if on a throne and took it for granted that we must worship. She seemed to feel certain of her own eminence. It is true, but it is rather crushing, for I feel she is very contemptuous of other people. When I stretched out a hand to feel another woman, I found only a very lovely, clear intellect. She does not seem to realize human beings as they are, but has a fantastic vision of them as strange birds or fishes

living in air or water in an unreal world. . . . She seems to come at full sail up to a subject one expects her to tackle and to combat and conquer the problem, but generally she evades the crucial moment. . . . Her eyes are like falcon's eyes and express so little. But she seems in some odd way more united than most of us, as if she never worried or troubled about anyone. She talked of her book *Night and Day*. The theme of it is that we all live in some dream world of our own with occasional rocks of real life emerging, but the dream is the ether round us. . . .

Ottoline Morrell was often ridiculed, because she took herself and her aspirations to an intellectual and poetic life very seriously indeed, with a sense of drama verging on the ludicrous. Also, she wore theatrical, extravagant clothes, huge hats, long dresses. But she was a woman of discernment and loyalty, and her assessment of Virginia Woolf's character is very perceptive indeed. For the great writer's slack grasp of reality was to weaken even more over the years. She was protected from the bouts of despair she suffered periodically – always after finishing a book – by her kind, unassuming and deeply honourable husband, Leonard Woolf, who had been a civil servant in the India Office. His memoirs have chronicled Bloomsbury's days with some charm. But even Leonard Woolf's attentiveness did not save Virginia. Capable of understanding with deep insight the rawness of a woman's sensibility, she was unable to fight her own hunger for self-destruction, and at the age of 59 killed herself by drowning in the stream at the bottom of her Sussex garden.

Vanessa, Virginia's sister, was a painter; her husband Clive Bell and his friend Roger Fry, the art critic and patron, continued the introduction in London of the work of the Continental Post-Impressionists, a process that had been interrupted by the War. Their exhibitions created a furore of indignation amongst the upholders of academic realism and classical draughtmanship (see plate 22). But although artists like Duncan Grant, and Vanessa Bell and Dora Carrington used a vibrant palette and experimented with great verve in forms and texture and patterning, they never achieved the greatness of their models across the

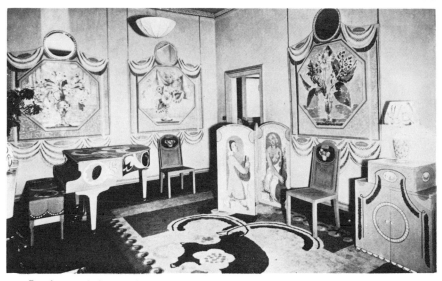

22. In the workshops of the Omega movement, Bloomsbury artists like Duncan Grant and Vanessa Bell applied their new vivid-coloured, geometric aestheticism to furniture, carpets and other everyday objects, as in this music room.

Channel – Bonnard, Vuillard, Matisse. What Bloomsbury did achieve was enthusiasm and support for artists prepared to break out of the expected mould of academic realist art. A vivid pictorial talent like that of Mark Gertler, a young artist from the Jewish East End, was encouraged by the interest and the responsiveness of the critics associated with Bloomsbury. Without them, he might not perhaps have been able to flourish as he did.

Bloomsbury also embraced the caustic essayist, Lytton Strachey (see colour plate 3), who poked fun at the generation of his grandfathers in his books *Eminent Victorians* and *Queen Victoria*, in which Florence Nightingale is a harridan and Queen Victoria tyrannical. The philosopher and mathematician, Bertrand Russell, later leader of the disarmament movement of the Sixties, also knew many of the people in Bloomsbury. But the circle only represented a tiny aspect of the richness of literature in the period.

The Twenties and early Thirties was the time when some of the most important works of the century were published, works which still embody what is meant by the modern spirit – the spirit that investigates the thought patterns of the psyche, the turbulence and the distress of modern man's relationship to society, that questions the nature of sexuality, that searches for God in a world that has renounced him or at best found him wanting.

Writing has not really broken new ground since then. That time saw the publication not only of Virginia Woolf's major novels, but of James Joyce's *Ulysses* (see plate 23), a difficult,

23 James Joyce, one of the many Irish writers who have enriched English literature, published his masterpiece, *Ulysses*, in 1922. He is photographed here by Berenice Abbot when he was suffering from the near blindness that affected his later years.

24. Augustus John was a celebrated painter for whom most of the distinguished men and women of the day posed. W. B. Yeats sat for these sketches in 1907, when the great Irish poet was 42 years old.

inventive narrative that interweaves, on a single day in Dublin, the lifetime of experiences and sensations of its two heroes, Leopold Bloom and Stephen Dedalus, and expresses them in a poetic, dream-like prose. *Ulysses* came out in 1922; E. M. Forster, a member of the Bloomsbury fringe, wrote what counts as perhaps his greatest novel, *Passage to India*, in 1924. Forster always chronicles his characters' behaviour with delicacy, against carefully evoked social backgrounds. In this novel, he shows subtle and penetrating sympathy with the mind of his Moslem hero Aziz, and so reveals the worlds of sensibility that separate him from Kipling. Kipling was still very much alive, but the older Edwardian and the Forster of the Twenties have nothing in common.

The poet W. B. Yeats (see plate 24), Irish patriot and restorer of Irish culture, was also writing all through these years. He died in 1939, aged 74. He has the headiest poetic imagination of the century. He first transmuted the myths and heroic figures of a pagan Ireland, then pursued a vision of salvation on this earth through beauty, the healing power of love, the enriching of memory through dreams and images. He expressed his lifelong quest with a quality of song that has not been surpassed in its powers of speaking straight to the soul in words of enchantment. In 1927, he wrote in despair of himself, as an old man for whom earthly pleasures were over. He dreams instead of a mind's voyage to the civilization he most associated with a wisdom and a splendour uncorrupted by time passing, the civilization of Byzantium:

An aged man is but a paltry thing,
A tattered coat upon a stick, unless
Soul clap its hands and sing, and louder sing
For every tatter in its mortal dress,
Nor is there singing school but studying
Monuments of its own magnificence;
And therefore I have sailed the seas and come
To the holy city of Byzantium.

O sages standing in God's holy fire
As in the gold mosaic of a wall,
Come from the holy fire, perne in a gyre,
And be the singing-masters of my soul.
Consume my heart away; sick with desire
And fastened to a dying animal
It knows not what it is; and gather me
Into the artifice of eternity.

Once out of nature I shall never take
My bodily form from any natural thing,
But such a form as Grecian goldsmiths make
Of hammered gold and gold enamelling
To keep a drowsy Emperor awake;
Or set upon a golden bough to sing
To lords and ladies of Byzantium
Of what is past, or passing, or to come.

Yeats deeply affected Irish national pride, because he founded the Abbey theatre in Dublin and revived so much of the country's cultural heritage, but he in no way illustrates the mood of the period; as an individual creative imagination, he stands right outside the literary fashions of his time.

Another poet, writing then though 23 years younger, captured the pessimism and the uprooted melancholy of the post-war generation in a society that was throwing away its chances of renewal. T. S. Eliot (see colour plate 5) was born American but lived and wrote all his life in England. He became a convinced Christian of the High Anglican persuasion, and this commitment filled his later poetry with a deep resignation and sense of the pervasiveness of sin through man's invincible weakness. His most famous poem, 'The Waste Land', was published in 1922; the 'Four Quartets' later. He is an illumination to read because his free-verse rhythms and juxtapositions of images, words, quotations work on the mind like prayer incantation, they stir pools of feeling mysteriously; his effect cannot really be fully understood. In 'The Waste Land' he describes the desolation of post-war London with characteristic melancholy:

> Unreal City,
> Under the brown fog of a winter dawn,
> A crowd flowed over London Bridge, so many,
> I had not thought death had undone so many.
> Sighs, short and infrequent, were exhaled,
> And each man fixed his eyes before his feet.

Possibly the most important figure of all novel writing in the Twenties was D. H. Lawrence (see plate 25). As a miner's son, he felt keen bitterness about social injustice, the unfulfilment of each man's greatness of soul. He saw that mere material improvements could not nurture the spiritual dimension he wished to see developed and satisfied in each individual; he pursued the idea of awakening men to self-knowledge all his life. But this pursuit meant a lifetime of contest for Lawrence – with society which he rejected, with his friends, most of whom he turned against at one time or another, with his country, which he left for exile abroad.

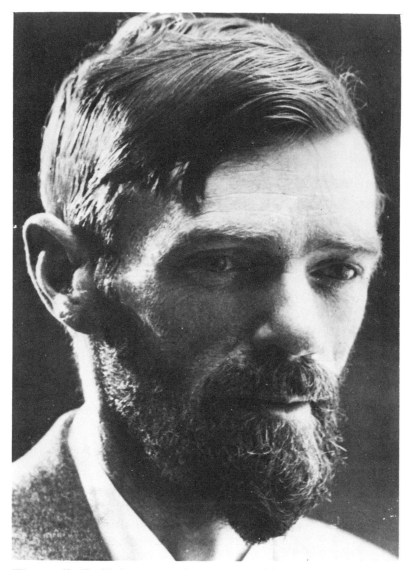

25. The novelist D. H. Lawrence, above, succeeded in communicating the power and the sacredness of passion between sexes. This has made him one of the century's most controversial writers.

He revolted in horror against the brutalization of the soul by the industrial conditions of work he had seen at first hand in his childhood and sought to return to what he considered was the natural state of man, in harmony with the physical side of his being and the physical order of creation. Like a monk who achieves understanding through long meditations on the essence of things, Lawrence observed the natural world carefully, evoking flowers and animals in his poetry with a brilliant eye. Of the kangaroo, he noticed, 'Her little loose hands and drooping Victorian shoulders . . .' and 'the long flat skis of her legs . . .'; of bats, he said they had 'wings like bits of umbrella. . . .' He wanted to restore factory man to his eyes and ears, to the senses, to the well-springs of his natural instincts.

His greatest novels, *Sons and Lovers, Women in Love* and *The Rainbow* were written before and during the War, but *The Rainbow* was at first suppressed, so that this masterpiece of passionate human observation was published only in 1929. Lawrence's scandalous reputation does him an injustice, for while he probes with ruthless curiosity the shifts and moods of human love, and while his search takes him naturally into the physical manifestations of love, he is a noble moralist, with a coherent viewpoint. In *The Rainbow* he investigates the pressure of family bonds between men and women, husbands and wives, fathers and daughters from generation to generation. He describes Anna Brangwen's restlessness, the restlessness of all adolescents:

> She was seventeen, touchy, full of spirits, and very moody: quick to flush, and always uneasy, uncertain. For some reason or other, she turned more to her father, she felt almost flashes of hatred for her mother. Her mother's dark muzzle and curiously insidious ways, her mother's utter surety and confidence, her strange satisfaction, even triumph, her mother's way of laughing at things and her mother's silent overriding of vexatious propositions, most of all her mother's triumphant power maddened the girl.
>
> She became sudden and incalculable. Often she stood at the window, looking out, as if she wanted to go. Sometimes she went, she mixed with people. But always she came home in anger, as if she were diminished, belittled, almost degraded. . . .
>
> Sometimes Anna talked to her father. She tried to discuss people, she wanted to know what was meant. But her father became uneasy.

He did not want to have things dragged into consciousness. Only out of consideration for her he listened. And there was a kind of bristling rousedness in the room. The cat got up and, stretching itself, went uneasily to the door. Mrs Brangwen was silent, she seemed ominous. Anna could not go on with her fault-finding, her criticism, her expression of dissatisfactions. She felt even her father against her. He had a strong, dark bond with her mother, a potent intimacy that existed inarticulate and wild, following its own course, and savage if interrupted, uncovered.

Nevertheless Brangwen was uneasy about the girl, the whole house continued to be disturbed. She had a pathetic, baffled appeal. She was hostile to her parents, even whilst she lived entirely within them, within their spell.

Many ways she tried, of escape.

Lawrence is always dragging into consciousness things that feel more comfortable left sleeping. He died comparatively young, at the age of 45, of tuberculosis, having suffered chronic ill health all his life. Rebecca West, herself a discerning mind and powerful author, maintained that he was constantly 'doing justice to the seriousness of life, and had been rewarded with a deeper insight into its nature than most of us have.'

Few people in the Twenties were aware of the books being written at the time. It often takes two decades at least to sift the writing of permanent value from amongst all the other books published at the same time. For most men and women in the Twenties Bloomsbury was simply a district in the heart of London, and Lawrence not even a name.

For the mass of English people the Twenties was the first decade of the mass media, spreading mass crazes. Popular culture exploded on the population. Radio, gramophone records, newspapers, fashions and fads flashed across the globe. Al Jolson, an American singer, crooned in the sitting rooms of the new secretary girls, records taught people to charleston or black bottom or foxtrot or swing to the new rhythms of jazz, they learnt to bob their hair and slash their skirt lengths, to leave off their stiff white collars and tailcoats and top hats and get into narrow pinstripes, flat boaters, soft trilbies (see plate 26). The

26. Edward Burra, with a merciless eye for human follies, drew these swells at the Ritz enjoying a cocktail in 1923, at the height of the time of the Bright Young Things.

plays and songs of Noel Coward, a polished, drawling, cool wit, caught the languor and the pleasure of the Twenties whirl. Coward satirizes the life-style of the Bright Young Things, in elegant pieces that have stood well the test of time. In *Private Lives* (see plate 27) and *Present Laughter* he also catches a new spirit, not exactly of classlessness, but of emancipation among the young which was the beginning of a true modern feeling. Evelyn Waugh, an impeccable stylist, turned the savage lamp of his intelligence on

27. Gertrude Lawrence (*right*) and Noel Coward (*left*), stars of the Twenties' line in elegant comedies, performed with the young Laurence Olivier (*right*) in Coward's sparkling play *Private Lives* (1930).

the hedonist society of the upper classes with their unthinking prejudices and their reckless self-love. In *Decline and Fall*, the hero, Paul Pennyfeather, is dumped trouserless in the fountain of his Oxford college by the young bloods who are, in Waugh's phrase, 'baying for broken glass'.

Techniques of mass production began however to erase differences of style between the classes' clothes – to some extent; the cinema disseminated the fashions of the most glamorous men and women in the world to thousands of viewers (see colour plate 6). Four thousand seven hundred cinemas were open by 1917. It was a hugely popular medium, purveying mainly American films. The English comic genius, Charlie Chaplin (see plate 28), the greatest of a long line of English clowns, reached through to everyone as, feet thrust out, bowler-hatted, black-suited and

28. Charlie Chaplin, seen here in *City Lights*, went to Hollywood and became the world's best-loved clown. But the comedies that he wrote, directed and acted often have a deeper side: *The Great Dictator*, about Hitler, and *Modern Times*, about factory life, are classics of the cinema.

moustachioed, he waddled through masterpieces like *The Gold Rush*, and, in the next decade, *Modern Times* and *The Great Dictator*.

Newspaper circulations soared: the rival giants of newspaper proprietors vied with each other for the biggest readerships. The

(a)

29. The daily life of
working people, especially
women's, was transformed
by relative advances in
household appliances, like
this 1906 vacuum cleaner
(a) and 1920 washing
machine (b).

(b)

Daily Express, owned by Lord Beaverbrook, won against the *Daily Mail* when its circulation topped two million in 1933. Everyone began doing crosswords, reading thrillers and detective stories. Agatha Christie became a best selling writer, and has remained so. Mass production and amenities lightened housework: vacuum cleaners, washing machines, man-made fibres, zip fasteners, electric irons, gas-fired heating and cooking, mangles, sanitary towels, and piped water in some areas of town all improved working conditions (see plate 29). This streamlining of the basic chores of household management, coupled with the emancipating influence of newspapers printing news of more liberated countries like the United States, carried forward the movement of women's independence. Yet this growing feeling was psychological, reflected more in the short skirts, make-up, and smoking habits of the Flapper – the young woman of the Twenties – than in visible economic changes (see plate 30). There were fewer women at work in 1921 than there had been before the war.

In other ways life began to resemble today in its conveniences and its attitudes. By 1930 there were, for instance, a growing number of cars – over a million – in private hands. The reformer, Marie Stopes, lectured on contraception in 1922; her book *Married Love* advised couples how to plan for the birth of their children. It pioneered the vital freedom to choose the size of one's family and helped make the use of contraceptives respectable. The BBC was founded – another, very important example of the spread of centralized state control, for here was the most potent means of communication so far invented in the hands of the Government. In 1929 the first experimental television programmes were broadcast, but at this stage there were few sets in people's homes. The material aspect of life was becoming recognizable, more like our own; and so, in a tragic way, was the stance of hopelessness, the feeling that nothing could be done that would make any difference.

Aldous Huxley, prophet of hopelessness, was one of a very gifted and clever family. A novelist and scientist, he published in 1923 *Antic Hay*, in which he captures the glitter of the 'Bright

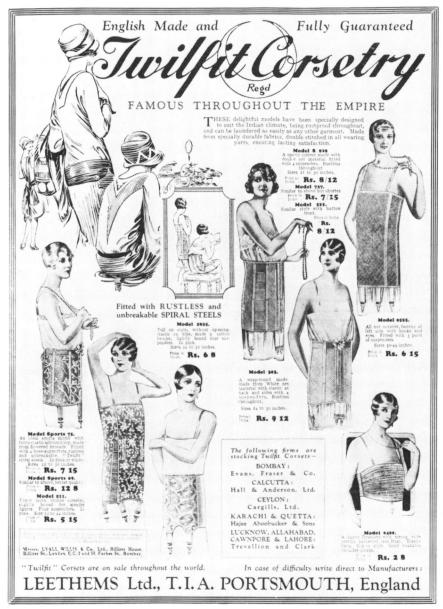

30. Women's shape follows fashion and fashion reflects social developments. In the 1920s, corsets, as seen in this contemporary advertisement, helped to create the boyish look of the new emancipated 'Flapper'.

Young Things' pleasures in the 1920s. His bored Bohemian set go to a nightclub, where an American jazz dance band is playing; and there, in the very midst of the giddy excitement of the senses, they wallow in the emptiness of their lives:

> At each recurrence of the refrain the four negroes of the orchestra, or at least the three of them who played with their hands alone – for the saxophonist blew at this point with a redoubled sweetness, enriching the passage with a warbling contrapuntal soliloquy that fairly wrung the entrails and transported the pierced heart – broke into melancholy and drawling song:
> 'What's he to Hecuba?
> Nothing at all.
> That's why there'll be no wedding on Wednesday week
> Way down in old Bengal.'
> 'What unspeakable sadness,' said Gumbril, as he stepped through the intricacies of the trot. 'Eternal passion, eternal pain . . . rum tiddle-um-tum, pom-pom. Amen. What's he to Hecuba? Nothing at all. Nothing, mark you. Nothing, nothing.'
> 'Nothing,' repeated Mrs Viveash. 'I know all about that.' She sighed.

While Huxley catches the despair in its hedonist setting, the mystical Yeats expressed it in the most intense prophecy of the decade, in words which still penetrate to the core of the twentieth century loss of faith:

> Turning and turning in the widening gyre
> The falcon cannot hear the falconer;
> Things fall apart; the centre cannot hold;
> Mere anarchy is loosed upon the world,
> The blood-dimmed tide is loosed, and everywhere
> The ceremony of innocence is drowned;
> The best lack all conviction, while the worst
> Are full of passionate intensity.

That is a fitting epitaph to the post-war period that began in such a flush of hope, with such proud promises on its lips.

🀫🀫🀫🀫🀫🀫

TEACH THE FREE MAN

🀫🀫🀫🀫🀫🀫

> With a firm grasp of half-truth, with political short-sight,
> With a belief we could disarm but at the same time fight,
> And that only the Left Wing could ever be right,
> And that Moscow, of all places, was the sole source of light:
>   Just like a young hopeful
>   Between the wars.
>
> WILLIAM PLOMER *Father and Son* 1939

IN Great Britain, the world financial crisis that followed the Crash of 1929 did not spawn a dictator: the English, in this, showed their extraordinary natural bent towards moderation. In Spain, in Italy, in Germany, men looked for extreme solutions. The worldwide depression in trade, the inflation of all currencies until haystacks of money notes were needed to buy the smallest items, widespread unemployment and little prospect of relief, all these circumstances made men look to desperate remedies, and revere those with the loudest mouths and the fiercest opinions. What Yeats had written in the Twenties was even more relevant in 1933:

> The best lack all conviction, while the worst
> Are full of passionate intensity.

Mussolini, Hitler, Franco, the three demagogues who seized power during the Thirties, in Italy, Germany and Spain respectively, were certain of the soundness of their vision and of their capacity to build a strong nation. Yet Italy and Germany were to be defeated in war; and Germany was to suffer as well the worst violence ever perpetrated by a nation against its own people, when

Hitler embarked on his programme to exterminate the Jews. Spain was to be torn apart by civil war, and afterwards, with Franco the victor, to endure forty years of repression of human rights.

Fascism, as practised by Hitler in Germany and his imitators elsewhere, meant that the individual – the 'little man' – counted for nothing, had no rights, no means of redress for wrongs, was the prey of the state authorities, from the top – the Leader himself – and from the bottom – the local policeman. Everyone was also at the mercy of the impersonal forces of the state, which were exalted by the heavy use of symbolism and pageantry, manipulated at will by the government. Fascism is characterized by the state control of all information, so that people only learn what their rulers wish them to think; and that limited and lying information was trumpeted abroad with the loudest use of official propaganda and the most lurid use of imagery. In Italy, Mussolini dressed up his followers, using the sinister glamour of black leather and black shirts to enhance their prestige. In Germany, the Swastika – an Oriental and ancient symbol of eternity – was debased to proclaim the power of the Fascist state on huge red banners hanging from every building and daubing every wall. In England, the Fascist leader, Oswald Mosley, copied Mussolini's black shirt uniforms. Men's minds can be controlled through images, and through the relentless repetition of them backed by threats and violence. No one has ever understood this process better than Hitler.

The effect of the rise of the dictators on England was rousing: the effete intellectual of the Twenties was shamed into action. The generation that had been spared the horrors of the First World War had grown up; it did not suffer from the lassitude and emotional exhaustion of its fathers. Poets like W. H. Auden, Stephen Spender (see plate 31), Louis MacNeice (see plate 39) and Cecil Day Lewis, and novelists like Christopher Isherwood (see plate 31), eagerly embraced the responsibility the artist has to the world. Gone was the day of the languid Bohemian caring nothing for the issues of the times; gone was the experimenter on the outer shores of society. Bloomsbury's preoccupations seemed

31. W. H. Auden, Christopher Isherwood, and Stephen Spender, photographed from left to right, by Howard Coster, were united in the Thirties by friendship and by a common purpose: to make literature effective in society and promote the Socialist revolution.

trivial and selfish. Writers confronted the moral and political problems at hand, and tried to come up with an answer. They were posturing to some extent, because later many recanted, saying their upper class backgrounds had made them feel guilty. But at the time they thought themselves sincere.

In England, the gravest problem was unemployment. The National Government merely trod water and hoped that the trouble would pass. It could find no solution; and the number of insured persons out of work climbed from 9 per cent of the total work force to 21·9 per cent in 1932 – 2·85 million people jobless. In 1933, the number went up to nearly 3 million insured people. And there were many thousands more out of work who were not insured. One of the few novels written by a man of the people at the time is Walter Greenwood's *Love on the Dole*, published in 1933. He describes life in a North Country industrial town hit by the slump. It is a poignant, simple, evocative book, underscoring heavily the shame of a society where families live dirty, over-crowded and hungry although they have worked all their lives, where only the pawnshop owner and the bookmaker have enough to eat, where a girl can only escape by prostituting herself to a richer man. The hero, Harry Hardcastle, has just been laid off:

> He felt icily alone.
>
> A tinge of shame coloured his cheeks; he licked his lips and slunk along by the walls. Then a burst of resentment swelled his heart. Didn't the people responsible know what this refusal to give him work meant to him?
>
> Didn't they know he now was a man? Didn't they know he wanted a home of his own? Didn't they know he'd served his time? Didn't they know he was a qualified engineer? Was he any concern of any-body's? Oh, what use was there in asking the air such questions. . . .

Northern towns, like Wigan in the coal-mining area, were scenes of desolation: men stood all day unoccupied, vacant, desperate, while women slaved at unprofitable occupations, trying to squeeze a little money from the less lean parts of the community, by taking in washing, or rag-picking. This landscape has been preserved for ever in the canvases of L. S. Lowry, a Northern naïve artist who turned to the belching factories and grim pavements of his chosen home in Salford for his subject matter. In painting after painting for over fifty years till his death in 1976, Lowry reduced the human figure to a scribble against a looming industrial sky, and so, although his images never truly developed, he remains a unique painter of ordinary working people's conditions (see plate 32).

George Orwell, essayist, novelist, polemicist, and the sharpest conscience of his day, lived for a time in Wigan in 1936. He describes the penury and misery of the people in his outraged book, *The Road to Wigan Pier*, and outlines the techniques of survival to which men resorted. He was present at the routine

32. L. S. Lowry remained gripped all his life by the landscape of his native Salford, and painted with a child-like lack of comment, the smokestacks, factory yards and street scenes of industrial life, as in this picture, *An Accident*.

theft of shale from the trucks of coaldust tipped up on to the slag heaps. In his diary he describes the scene:

> ... not less than 100 men, a few boys, waiting, each with a sack and coal hammer strapped under his coat tails. Presently the train hove in sight, coming round the bend at about 20 m.p.h. Fifty or seventy men rushed for it, seized hold of the bumpers, etc., and hoisted themselves into the trucks. It appears that each truck is regarded as the property of the men who have succeeded in getting onto it while it is moving. The engine ran the trucks up onto the dirt-heap, uncoupled them and came back for the remaining trucks. There was the same wild rush and the second train was boarded in the same manner ... the men on top began shovelling the stuff out to their women and other supporters below, who rapidly sorted out the dirt and put all the coal (a considerable amount but all small, in lumps about the size of eggs) into their sacks....

George Orwell was deeply concerned all his life about the condition of the common man; in this, he was a true child of the Thirties. An Etonian, he first became a police inspector, a government servant in the Burmese colonial office. But writing was his greatest love, and his fine, exceptional and very high-minded sense of fairness led him to some of the most powerful political writing this century. He was wholly committed to the cause of socialism, which he saw as the only remedy for the grinding inequality epitomized in Wigan. He stuck to this solution all his life, but he was incapable of dishonesty, and could not gloss over the problems, or disguise the crimes and shortcomings of which the left-wing was guilty. For instance, in *Homage to Catalonia*, one of his masterpieces, Orwell describes his role in the Spanish Civil War. In 1936 War broke out in Spain between the elected Republican Government and the forces of General Franco who aimed to take over and abolish the democratic regime the Republicans had declared. Orwell was one of a number of intellectuals from other countries in Europe who was so appalled at this assault on an established government and so outraged by the help given to Franco by the Fascist countries, and by the indifference and inaction of the British Government, that he joined up, fighting in a small Anarchist group on the Republican side. He was present in Barcelona when fighting broke out between the Communists and the Anarchists, who were meant to be comrades-in-arms defending freedom together. His account of the battle in the streets, the struggles and the violence, illuminates the horrors of intrigue that often destroy the idealism of political parties. Orwell himself remained true to his left-wing convictions, but he was too much a writer, and too little a propagandist to fight shy of telling the truth; the paradoxical result has been that his works have provided ammunition against left-wing causes.

Later, his astonishing tours de force, *Animal Farm*, and *1984*, unmasked the totalitarian horrors of the Communist regime in Russia with a brutal sense of wit and a searing use of allegory. They are the most important works of political fiction in the twentieth century, and their message remains true of the despotic regimes that now control an even greater part of the globe than they did when Orwell was writing. Orwell always defended the freedom of the individual against encroachments from left and right but often his was a solitary and courageous voice.

Most intellectuals in the Thirties were too possessed by the hope that Communism would provide the answer to confront the truth: that Stalin, the Russian leader, was turning the country into one vast concentration camp, killing off all those who refused to co-operate with his designs and massacring thousands of peasants who resisted the Government's efforts to collectivize their land into 'soviets'.

But because the decade of the Thirties saw the success of Fascism, many clever and influential men took up the cause of Communism as a riposte to the threat of Hitler. The theory was sound: Communism argued that power and money, the means of production and its fruits, should be in the hands of the people who toiled, the people who were the producers of wealth; Fascism on the other hand maintains state capitalism, concentrating power and money in the hands of a few big government-controlled leaders. In practice, twentieth century experience has proved this contrast false. Right-wing and left-wing dictatorships often resemble each other closely. In the Thirties this was not as apparent as it is now, and Orwell was then one of the few men to see the problem. He wrote *Animal Farm*, a savage satire about the Stalinist purges, and it is a very illuminating epitaph to the period, that it was turned down by several publishers because it painted the events in Russia too black. The book was not published until 1945. This was not because English publishers are deceivers; but because they were deceived. They too were bitten with the bug of wishful thinking.

For the Thirties was the decade of wishful thinking. Its testimony lives on, a forlorn reminder of the hopes intelligent men can entertain – against all the odds. The writers were full of optimism. In an important anthology, *New Country*, published in 1933, the editor Michael Roberts exhorted writers to take up contemporary issues: 'If your writing about a new world is to mean more than buttercup lyricism, you must know how that world is to come into being and precisely what sort of a world it will be.' He asked literary men to become prophets. In the book, the predominant note is intoxicated optimism: the revolution is about to bring justice and equality to England. One contributor, the poet

A. S. J. Tessimond, hymned the advancing new age, using the image of the aeroplane, which was then an equally revolutionary modern phenomenon:

There's also my civilization. . . .
              somewhere, arriving:
The plane long delayed, behind schedule some centuries,
              Held up by cloudbanks,
A strut or two broken – but coming: my civilization advancing
When a man gains his claim to work, shirk, without spies
              At the windows,
Whenever minorities win (though majorities steal their slogans),
Whenever a censor's shamed, or an inquisitor abolished.

The greatest mind who embraced left-wing idealism, the most potent imagination and ardent genius, was that of W. H. Auden. He died only recently, after a lifetime's quest for solutions to mankind's illnesses through poetry. He was a great poet, with a musician's ear, a dazzling wizardry with language and imagery, and a constant ability to handle ideas at an intellectual level without losing the beauty of line and image that is essential in poetry. His genius had unusual roots: in his descent from the Norsemen or Vikings, which made him love northern landscapes, especially the glaciers and volcanoes of Iceland, and also in his early training as a scientist. In the Twenties, he visited Berlin and was converted to the cause of anti-Fascism by his understanding of what life was to be like under Hitler. His colleague and friend Christopher Isherwood has described the decadence and the indifference of Berlin during Hitler's rise to power that he and Auden both witnessed in his famous short stories *Goodbye to Berlin* (1939) and the novel *Mr Norris Changes Trains*. The casual way in which Germans accepted the growing atrocities around them still chills the marrow as one reads Isherwood's spare description of Nazis beating someone up in public.

Another passer-by and myself were the first to reach the doorway where the young man was lying. He lay huddled crookedly in the corner, like an abandoned sack. As they picked him up, I got a sickening glimpse of his face – his left eye was poked half out, and blood poured from the wound. He wasn't dead. Somebody volunteered to take him to the hospital in a taxi.

By this time, dozens of people were looking on. They seemed surprised, but not particularly shocked – this sort of thing happened too often, nowadays. . . .

It is a mark of Auden's generous spirit that, faced with such horrors as these, he turned to a romantic Marxism and hoped to find in it an answer. He wrote:

> Comrades to whom our thoughts return,
> Brothers for whom our bowels yearn
> When words are over;
> Remember that in each direction
> Love outside our own election
> Holds us in unseen connection:
> O trust that ever.

A mark of generosity, yes, but not entirely of good sense. Auden was to regret later the partisanship of his feelings. In a 1977 autobiography, *Christopher and His Kind*, Isherwood, his companion, dismissed the whole love affair with Communism as a sham. 'They had been playing parts, repeating slogans created for them by others. . . .' With these words, he betrays his friend's lifelong efforts to believe in something that would provide relief for the world's ills.

It was an effort which took Auden to Spain in 1936 to try and take part – unsuccessfully as it turned out – in the Republican struggle; and to China later in 1937 to report the Japanese attempt to subdue the Chinese by violence. Auden was sincere when he sang out for Marxism; just as he was when he later proclaimed his renewed faith in Christianity. To say he was not is to fail to understand the times when every right-thinking man had to feel himself committed to a just cause. Auden's fundamental belief was in the basic honesty of each person, and his need for his natural eloquence to speak out from the heart. One of his most famous poems, written in 1939 to commemorate the death

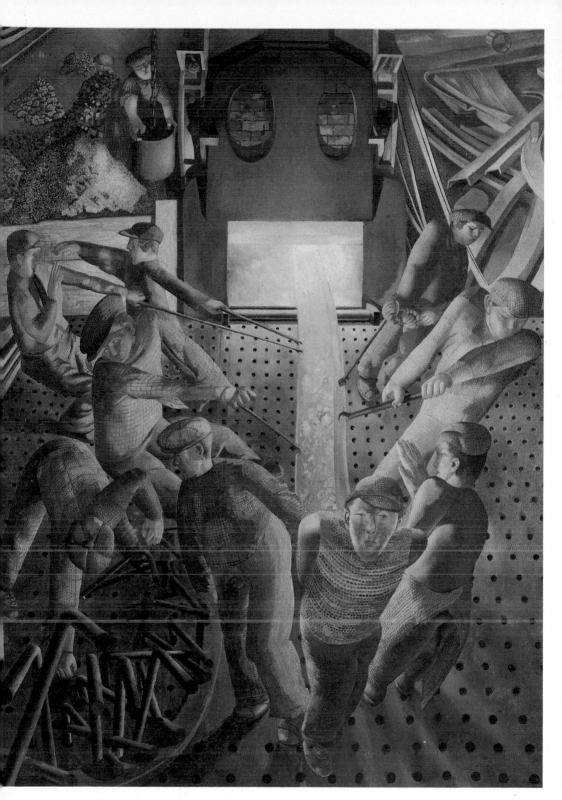

7. During World War II, Stanley Spencer served as a war artist, and produced the magnificent sequence, *Shipbuilding on the Clyde* (detail above). He is more famous for the private metaphysical visions centred on his home village of Cookham in the Thames Valley.

8. Each Trade Union branch has its own banner, often a beautiful and imaginative piece of propaganda art worked in embroidery and paint. Here Dan Jones captures the rousing pageantry of a big demonstration against the imprisonment of five dockers in Pentonville.

of the greatest of contemporary poets, W. B. Yeats, ends with a
plea that society should let each man have a free tongue:

> Earth, receive an honoured guest:
> William Yeats is laid to rest.
> Let the Irish vessel lie
> Emptied of its poetry.
>
> In the nightmare of the dark
> All the dogs of Europe bark,
> And the living nations wait,
> Each sequestered in its hate;
>
> Intellectual disgrace
> Stares from every human face,
> And the seas of pity lie
> Locked and frozen in each eye.
>
> Follow, poet, follow right
> To the bottom of the night,
> With your unconstraining voice
> Still persuade us to rejoice;
>
> With the farming of a verse
> Make a vineyard of the curse,
> Sing of human unsuccess
> In a rapture of distress;
>
> In the deserts of the heart
> Let the healing fountain start,
> In the prison of his days
> Teach the free man how to praise.

Often, the people who held Communist sympathies were also
pacifists. War, it was thought, was the result of big business or of
capitalist arms manufacturers seeking to increase their profits and
working in collaboration with imperialists who wanted to subdue
other nations into serfdom for their own interests. There was a
widespread outcry, throughout the pre-war period, against the
rising manufacture of armaments by government contractors.
Arms, by their very existence, led to war, it was believed –

certainly one can say that the nature of the arms manufactured determines the nature of the war that follows.

The poet, Julian Bell, son of Clive and Vanessa Bell of Bloomsbury, who fought and died in the Spanish Civil War, poured sarcasm on the arms race:

> Thus nations grow secure, with endless bother,
> By each being twice as strong as every other, . . .
> But only for defence, we all insist,
> Each still is armed each other to resist,
> And for defence superior force prepares,
> And no one contemplates offensive wars.

In practice, British expenditure on defence reached an all time low in the budget introduced by Neville Chamberlain in 1932. Public opinion ranged against war, and was not outraged by the weakening of British might. Nor could the economy afford anything else. Disarmament was thus not a result of policy but of inability to do much else.

In the thirties the ideas of intellectuals found a new revolutionary channel of communication: the cheap book. Penguin started publishing sixpenny paperbacks in 1935, and many of the titles had a socialist content (see plate 33). In May, 1936, by a stroke of inspiration, Victor Gollancz, the publisher, hit upon the idea of a subscription club, the members of which would receive a monthly book at a very low price. The Left Book Club, publishing many eminent left-wing writers and reports, was a unique feature of the late Thirties. It produced Edgar Snow's classic study of Chinese Communism, *Red Star over China*, a miner's firsthand account of his experiences – B. L. Coombes' *These Poor Hands* – as well as the future Prime Minister Clement Attlee's analysis *The Labour Party in Perspective*, and George Orwell's *The Road to Wigan Pier*. The club commanded the huge circulation of fifty thousand, and thus gave a much wider currency to hitherto exclusive ideas.

But the turbulent currents of intellectual thought had very little effect, it can safely be said, on the behaviour or plans of politicians. The Labour Party remained centrist, and continued to disaffiliate itself from Communism. None of the country's

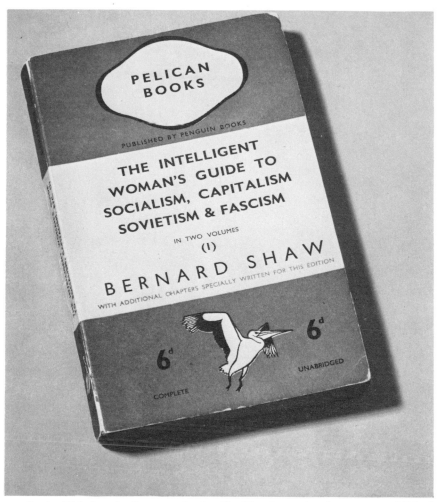

33. In the Thirties, the first paperbacks, like Shaw's treatise above, were published at six old pence each. Their availability was a major social revolution.

leaders sympathized with Communist struggles against Fascism.

Fascism was certainly considered an enemy – the British brand of it, started by the renegade Socialist, Sir Oswald Mosley, declined after 1937, when new laws were passed to stop its disgusting and systematic use of mob violence (see plate 34). But regarding matters abroad, the Government was not prepared to risk a firm stand. In 1935, economic sanctions banning imports from

34. The Fascist movement gained little support in England. Ugly demonstrations, like this 1937 outbreak, fanned anti-semitism in London's East End until a law was passed banning them.

Italy and some exports were used to try and prevent an Italian conquest of Abyssinia by force. The sanctions were unsuccessful. Nothing at all was done to prevent Japan's invasion of China and the protracted war on Chinese territory. As for the Civil War in Spain, there was a general agreement amongst other countries not to intervene with aid or arms.

In English society circles, there was a great deal of covert admiration for the dictators and their system. Mosley, himself a member of the upper classes and a man of brilliance and charm, helped disguise the brutalities of Fascism by his unabashed admiration of Hitler. Mussolini made the trains run on time, it was said, and this was good enough for the Italians. Hitler was restoring Germany's strength as if by a miracle – even the military threat of such a resurgence did not altogether wipe out admiration of his achievement. In this respect, the British aristocracy showed yet again their deplorable natural bent towards imperialism: what they would not tolerate at home for one moment was quite all right for foreigners.

On the domestic front politics during the decade of the Thirties were humdrum. Ramsay MacDonald retired, an old man, in 1935, and, in one of the most egalitarian gestures of his career, refused to accept a peerage. Stanley Baldwin succeeded him as Prime Minister. His third spell in office was disrupted by the juiciest scandal of the Thirties, the abdication of King Edward VIII in 1936. The king wanted to marry Wallis Simpson, a married American who had already been divorced once. With his beloved, he moved in a whirl of cocktail parties, yachting holidays in the Mediterranean and all-night club crawls. One diarist of the period, Marie Belloc Lowndes, described seeing Mrs Simpson at a dinner party:

> She was very much made up with what I would call a Red Indian colouring, that is, yellow and brick-red. . . . She wore a very great deal of jewellery, which I thought must be what is called 'dressmaker's' jewels, so large were the emeralds in her bracelets and so striking and peculiar a necklace.

. . . Later, of course, Mrs Lowndes discovered that 'all the jewels were real, that the then Prince of Wales had given her fifty thousand pounds' worth at Christmas, following it up with sixty thousand pounds' worth of jewels a week later at the New Year.'

The King was hounded from the throne by respectable opinion, voiced most strongly by the Prime Minister himself. Edward VIII thus became the last personification of the romantic hero of the fairy tale romance, the king who gives up his kingdom for love. Yet the lives of the Duke and Duchess of Windsor, as the king and Mrs Simpson then became, seemed sad and empty. Obsessed with a sense of grievance against England, enamoured of the worst kind of rich pleasure-loving and often right-wing company, interested more in clothes than in anything else, the couple idled away a life of exile until the Duke of Windsor's death in 1972.

Baldwin, the steadiest of men, thus had to deal with two unique upheavals in his career: the General Strike of 1926, and the Abdication of 1936. Otherwise he continued prudently and surely as Prime Minister, never doing anything very dangerous. Most importantly, he began the process of rearmament, because the economy improved and he cared nothing for the opinion of intellectuals and pacifists. Neville Chamberlain, who succeeded him as Prime Minister in 1938, was described by a contemporary, Sir Robert Bruce Lockhart, as 'cold and clammy as a dead trout'. He continued the policy of cautious re-armament against the threat of Hitler, but he tried to neutralize the threat by negotiation. This policy, which took Chamberlain many times to Germany to plead for peace with the Fuhrer in person, was called Appeasement. It seemed successful at the time, and Chamberlain was greatly admired by the British, who were very anxious not to be involved in another major war against Germany. But while Britain appeased, Hitler annexed by invasion and conquest the neutral and sovereign countries of Austria and Czechoslovakia. When he entered Poland, the British could no longer allow his aggressions. War was declared on 3rd September, 1939.

What broke the idealism of the artists and writers of the Thirties was not only the inevitable decline into a new, terrible war caused by Hitler's campaign of European conquest. The greater shock was the Nazi-Soviet pact of 23rd August, 1939, by which communist and fascist promised not to attack each other. This cynical sinking of principles for the sake of aggrandizement marks a turning point in the history of the twentieth century. It was impossible from then on to believe that when expediency dictated the opposite, vaunted ideals would still underpin the actions of a revolutionary government.

Auden and Isherwood became completely disillusioned. They gave up the fight. Auden decided to leave England to live in the United States. He did so in January 1939, foreseeing the failure of his hopes. There he remained until he settled down in a backwater in the Austrian mountains. Their exile symbolized the defeat of the decade. Auden became convinced that writers could not affect history or politics one jot. What had begun as a vast aspiration towards a new world, ended with the outbreak of war, in a sense of futility. Auden wrote:

> The social and political history of Europe would be just the same if Shakespeare, Dante and Goethe had never written. The only people who affect the political climate are journalists who try and produce the truth, and writers in countries where there is no freedom – so any statement from any writer carries weight. But the poet is really like Dr Johnson: 'I write a little better to endure the world and a little better to enjoy it.'

It is a disputable view, as the enduring influence of George Orwell alone makes plain. But for Auden it seemed true, because the political commitment of writers in the Thirties achieved so little.

🔁🔁🔁🔁🔁🔁

EASY MAKING GHOSTS

🔁🔁🔁🔁🔁🔁

> For every static world that you and I impose
> Upon the real one must crack at times and new
> Patterns from old disorders open like a rose
> And old assumptions yield to new sensation;
> The Stranger in the wings is waiting for his cue,
> The fuse is always laid to some annunciation.
> LOUIS MACNEICE *Mutations*

IN the Autumn of 1940, George Orwell, the most forthright and forceful voice of the Left in England, spoke out his commitment to the war against Nazism in no uncertain terms. Only by fighting Hitler would the longed-for Socialist revolution in England arrive. Orwell lashed out, by implication, at the intellectuals and the artists who remained aloof or pacifist, or who had, like Auden, vanished to America. He wrote:

> What I knew in my dream that night was that the long drilling in patriotism which the middle classes go through had done its work, and that once England was in a serious jam it would be impossible for me to sabotage. But let no one mistake the meaning of this. Patriotism has nothing to do with conservatism. . . . Only revolution can save England, that has been obvious for years, but now the revolution has started, and it may proceed quite quickly if only we can keep Hitler out. Within two years, maybe a year, if only we can hang on, we shall see changes that will surprise the idiots who have no foresight. I daresay the London gutters will have to run with blood. All right, let them, if it is necessary. But when the red militias are billeted in the Ritz, I shall still feel that the England I was taught to love so long ago and for such different reasons is somehow persisting.

Orwell's toughness and his tender protectiveness towards England is entirely characteristic of the early years of the war. A wave of powerful emotion swept over the country, washing away the apathy and the idleness on the one side, the pacifism and intellectual internationalism on the other that had marked the previous decade. In a matter of months, Neville Chamberlain, hitherto lauded for his diplomatic manoeuvres to avoid war, found himself reviled for failing to be warlike, for failing to get Britain prepared for war, for failing to promote the re-arming of the forces. During the first year of the Second World War, there was only uneasy fighting, as Hitler appeared to be treading water. But then Denmark and Norway fell, and at home, the crisis around Chamberlain's leadership grew. Chamberlain, neat, polite, and lustreless, was a man of the Thirties; his successor, Winston Churchill, was indeed the personification of the new spirit abroad, the spirit of wartime England.

Churchill was old in 1940 – 66 years old – with thirty years of public life behind him. He had sat in the Cabinet *before* the First World War. His had been one of the stormiest of twentieth century political careers, suffering one eclipse after another. He changed parties twice, adopted unpopular stands; yet also stood for belligerence, the pride of empire, the ancient glory of Britain. As First Lord of the Admiralty, he dreamed up the attack on Gallipoli in the First World War, extending the fighting with ghastly consequences. His joy in hardware was unbounded: he liked to sail in his own battleship around England's shores, inspecting naval installations. W. H. Auden captured Churchill's attitude in his satirical poem, 'A Happy New Year':

> Churchill was speaking of a battleship:
> It was some little time before I had guessed
> He wasn't describing a woman's breast.

He often took a fiercely isolated view; he opposed, for instance, the granting of concessions towards an independent India in 1931, and left the Conservative Shadow Cabinet over the matter. He was one of the few eminent figures to support Edward VIII over his desire to marry Mrs Simpson. He took a firm stand against the women's vote. Yet in some ways he was progressive: he understood the need for government control of the economy in wartime, and had already supported socialist measures along these lines during the First World War. He was an inveterate scribbler, an obsessive talker, loving orotund speeches that he delivered in the hugely eloquent rasping and virile tone that was to become so familiar and so uplifting to English people through the radio during the Second World War. Churchill did most things to excess: from the consumption of brandy and cigars, to, eventually, the bombing of German cities. His excesses had brought him ignominy often enough – for a man of undoubtedly towering gifts, he had an extraordinarily chequered career – but they were exactly what the public wanted after war broke out. Churchill was carried to the premiership in 1940 not by the love of his colleagues in either party (for most had little cause to love his persistent tendency to maverick behaviour) but by a genuine democratic surge of trust in him and desire for his leadership, which the politicians recognized, and to which they yielded when he was made leader of the Conservative Party and Prime Minister. Marie Belloc Lowndes, in her diary of 1941, recalled:

> the astonishing change which has taken place with regard to the general view now held of Churchill. During the year when he was in the wilderness I was often the only one in a considerable company to say a good word for him. It was grudgingly admitted that he wrote very well: that he was very clever, but always he was labelled as 'dangerous', 'impulsive', and the last man who ought once more to play any part in public affairs.
>
> Then in 1940 he was treated as a saviour. If people said a word of criticism concerning any action of his, he or she was regarded as a traitor. Apparently, he accepted the adulation lavished on him with simple good humour. . . .

The figure of Churchill, massive, bullish, chin thrust forward, mouth grimly set to defy all foes, seemed to stand as a bulwark between England and the danger that threatened her. The more terrible the menace, the more imposing did Churchill's bulk

35. Churchill took charge of the war with the country's enthusiastic support in 1940. Here Illingworth caricatures the 'saviour of his country's' love of personal intervention, for Churchill liked to fly all over the war zone himself.

appear. He became, for the English people, a new Britannia. He personified their pluck (see plate 35).

The second phase of the War began in April, 1940, when Germany invaded and conquered Belgium and the Lowlands, then swept on to France, secured her surrender in June, and drove the British army back on to the shores of Normandy. Their only

36. Firefighters worked nightly in London and other big cities and ports against the Blitz. Unlike in the First World War, civilians in the Second suffered the fighting at first hand.

refuge then became fishing smacks and pleasure craft from the South Coast of England in the great evacuation of Dunkirk. But Dunkirk, the horror of defeat and yet the glory of the little man's defiance and escape, rallied the English people more effectively than any victory. At the same time, the spring of 1940, the Germans' Luftwaffe began bombing English cities. The Blitz, as it was called after the German word for a lightning attack, Blitzkrieg, had an extraordinary effect on British morale: far from inspiring despair, it roused the population to heights of patriotic endeavour and self-sacrifice.

The suffering of civilians during the air-raids (see plate 36), their witness of the destructive forces that previously only troops in combat had seen, made the experience of the Second World War completely different from that of the First. This difference was expressed in the writing and arts of the time. There were few war poets describing the front line ordeal, compared with the number there had been during the First World War. The cleavage between soldier and civilian was not so pronounced. The men and women who stayed at home were able to participate in the horror of the war – in a different way, of course, but with enough emotion to feel themselves to be combatants too.

The poets who remained in England were transformed by the experience of bombing. Edith Sitwell (see plate 37), an

37. Edith Sitwell represented, with her two brothers Osbert and Sacheverell, a high, worthy but rather precious attitude to art. She is photographed here by Cecil Beaton with his characteristic sense of interior décor.

To Willie Walton
from
Kit Wood
Dec. 1925

38. William Walton formed part of the renaissance of British music. Here he is drawn as a young man by the artist Christopher Wood, who died at the age of 29, before he could consolidate his exciting early work.

elegant, weird poet was much painted and photographed for the exotica of her jewels and turbans and costumes and the idiosyncrasy of her long, cadaverous face with its bird-of-prey nose and monumental forehead. Before the War, she and her two brothers, Osbert and Sacheverell, formed the centre of an artistic society devoted to the avant-garde in art. She collaborated with the composer William Walton (see plate 38) on his vital, amusing work, 'Façade', for which she wrote tone-poems, witty fantasies using a rich, dream-like vocabulary. But the war stripped the frivolity and the exquisiteness from her poetic diction and gave her a huge, profound theme to work on. She undertook an epic, 'The Shadow of Cain', about the war, and she mined the imagery of Christianity to describe the apocalyptic effect of its violence. A shorter, more famous poem, 'Still Falls the Rain', describes an air-raid over London, as if it were the Crucifixion taking place again.

Still falls the Rain
With a sound like the pulse of the heart that is changed to the hammer-beat
In the Potter's Field, and the sound of the impious feet

On the Tomb:
    Still falls the Rain
In the Field of Blood where the small hopes breed and the human brain
Nurtures its greed, that worm with the brow of Cain.

Still falls the Rain
At the feet of the Starved Man hung upon the Cross.
Christ that each day, each night, nails there,
have mercy on us –
On Dives and on Lazarus:
Under the Rain the sore and the gold are as one

Still falls the Rain –

For the most part the poets of the Twenties and Thirties forgot their pessimism and their hatred of English society's traditions, and joined up to do war work as best they could. Some were too old for active service, some preferred to avoid it. Most found themselves other duties. Stephen Spender did not follow his great friends, Auden and Isherwood, to America, but his earlier revolutionary feelings were subdued. He stayed in England as a fire-watcher, and one of his most arresting poems describes an air-raid over Plymouth. The lessons of the Thirties have not been forgotten: he uses the images of commonplace life and draws on daily experience to evoke vividly the searchlights picking out the enemy planes in the sky above the vulnerable harbour and its precious naval base.

Above the whispering sea
And waiting rocks of black coast,
Across the bay, the searchlight beams
Swing and swing back across the sky.

Their ends fuse in a cone of light
Held for an instant up
Until they break away again
Smashing that image like a cup. . . .

Triangles, parallels, parallelograms,
Experiment with hypotheses
On the blackboard sky,
Seeing that X
Where the enemy is met.
Two beams cross
To chalk his cross.

A sound, sounding ragged, unseen
Is chased by two swords of light.
A thud. An instant when the whole night gleams.
Gold sequins shake out of a black-silk screen.

Louis MacNeice (see plate 39), Spender's contemporary, and once a kindred voice in the radical poets' movement of the Thirties, returned to England to take part in the war effort after a cry of protest had gone up about Auden and Isherwood's seeming defection or despair. He joined the BBC, which played a crucial role in stimulating the British spirit under the stress of the Blitz and the long struggle of the six years of war. MacNeice was a

9. Francis Bacon's work distills the contemporary sense of futility and pain. This 1950 *Fragment of a Crucifixion* is one of many versions in which Bacon tackles the most enduring symbol of suffering in our culture.

10. Lucien Freud, another of the greatest living English painters, expresses a similar violent pessimism. His *Girl With White Dog* (1950-1) emphasizes the haunted appearance of the human figure by the pallor of the animal's coat.

11. *A Bigger Splash*, one of a sequence of swimming pool paintings made in California, is a famous work of the young and hugely successful artist David Hockney.

39. Louis MacNeice, photographed here by the Cambridge professor E. R. Dodds, is one of Britain's most interesting, lucid and attractive poets. Since his death in 1963, his work has not been as widely read as it should.

Protestant from Northern Ireland, the son of a bishop. He became a schoolmaster himself and a poet of lucid intelligence and sanity, meditative, prudent, sensitive to the vast panoply of moral choice that faces each man on earth and the enormous difficulties it poses. He is on the whole, therefore, a pessimistic poet, but the degree of human sympathy in his work redeems him from Eliot's greater resignation and love of emptiness. He is also a very witty poet, adept at the English language's byways and flexibility. Around 1943, when most of the City of London had been razed, and coastal towns very badly damaged, MacNeice wrote a marvellous poem about the fires in London after bombings, a poem of chill, bright images, hard with savagery and the excitement of destruction: he called it ironically, in a reminiscence of St Francis's hymn to creation, 'Brother Fire':

> When our brother Fire was having his dog's day
> Jumping the London streets with millions of tin cans
> Clanking at his tail, we heard some shadow say
> 'Give the dog a bone' – and so we gave him ours;
> Night after night we watched him slaver and crunch away
> The beams of human life, the tops of topless towers. . . .
>
> O delicate walker, babbler, dialectician Fire,
> O enemy and image of ourselves,
> Did we not on those mornings after the All Clear,
> When you were looting shops in elemental joy
> And singing as you swarmed up city block and spire,
> Echo your thought in ours? 'Destroy! Destroy!'

The Blitz provided what the Trenches had done in the First World War: the knowledge of horror shared equally. This inspired the poets, and also freed them – for a time – from the aching anxiety most of them had felt throughout the inter-war years about the intellectuals' proper role in English society. They could record the fires, the deaths, the holocaust of English cities with a firm commitment against murder wherever it may occur. One poet, Stevie Smith, who was never identified with any movement in her lifetime, decided that the tragedy of war was too great to write about, that its sufferings should be given the respect of silence, as one pays at a graveside to remember the dead. Stevie Smith is a bizarre poetic voice, inimitable though deceptively simple, possessor of an artless, whimsical, melancholy and ingenious imagination with astonishing technical abilities to extract humour from rhyme and rhythm. She illustrated her poems with dry doodles, often of herself as an apprehensive, wistful child. But she did depart from her resolve to ignore the war in one, highly characteristic poem:

It was my bridal night I remember,
An old man of seventy-three
I lay with my young bride in my arms,
A girl with T.B.
It was wartime, and overhead
The Germans were making a particularly heavy raid on Hampstead.
What rendered the confusion worse, perversely,
Our bombers had chosen that moment to set out for Germany.
Harry, do they ever collide?
I do not think it has ever happened,
Oh my bride, my bride.

Unlike the writers, the artists were organized by the State and were given employment, the most valuable gift of all, to record the war according to their personal vision. The War Artists Advisory

40. Albert Richards, who painted this picture, *The Landing*, was killed in 1945 on active service as a War Artist.

Committee was set up and chaired by Kenneth Clark, then the young director of the National Gallery and a patron – on behalf of the State – of genius. The WAAC kept alive and working most of the best artists in England then. Many of them had not had commissions on this scale before the War and indeed had won no recognition of their importance at all. The War Artists (see plate 40 and colour plate 7) were either commissioned into the forces as officers, and then left to paint and draw their experiences, or, in the case of those too old to serve, were sent to different places in England to set down the civilian experience of war. Masterpieces have resulted from this brilliant experiment in state patronage of the arts – a unique achievement. Henry Moore, the greatest sculptor England has produced since the craftsmen of Wells and Lincoln cathedrals, was in his forties during the War. As a War Artist, he became absorbed in the subterranean life of the underground tunnels in London, that flowered spontaneously into a new community, as thousands of people flocked to sleep there in shelter from the Blitz (see plate 41). Henry Moore filled sketchbooks with drawings of the blanketed, draped figures lying in groups on the platforms, sitting ranked side by side on the benches, mothers and babies huddled, families wrapped under miscellaneous blankets. His personal understanding of the family of man, as expressed by individual groups, captured the distress of the bombed-out folk of London's poor (it was mostly the poor who used the Underground for shelter) as something monumental, dignified, an epic experience in the context of simple human emotions – survival, family love, resignation. The drawings, which are now justly famous, also developed many of the aesthetic images which Moore later sculpted: the reclining, swathed torsoes, the family groups, the enthroned, majestic solitary figures seated side by side – all these were later to appear transformed into the imposing proportions of his sculpture and its weighty acceptance of the ordinary dignity of life: he has carved and cast many mothers and children, kings and queens, reclining nudes. The experience of the shelters was a seminal one for Moore. His prodigious energy had given birth to an enormous opus in stone and wood before the War, and his genius had been

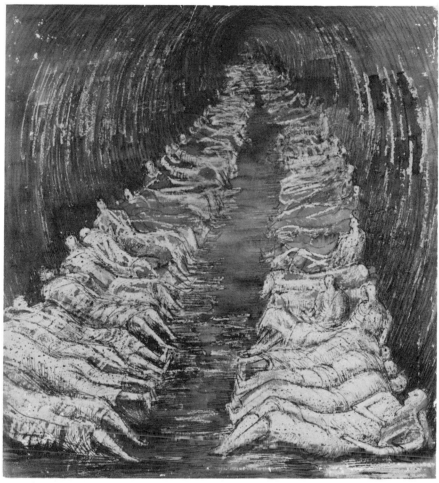

41. Henry Moore made a long sequence of sketches in the uncompleted under-ground system in London, where families took shelter during the air raids. The drawings mark an important development in Moore's treatment of the human form, the central image of his sculpture.

recognized by a few discerning artists and critics, like Clark himself and Roland Penrose. But his material life was a struggle, and many notices of his exhibitions had sneered at his forms for ugliness and meaninglessness. With his war work, he was able to reach a much increased audience, and to accustom the public to a new vision, for the WAAC commissions were displayed widely and were remarkably popular.

Other painters, who had pursued their work within the limited scope of the philistine climate of the inter-war years, also now found expression for their talents in the mainstream of public life. Clark has remarked that his Committee enabled painters 'to go on painting with a clear conscience. . . .' This was true of many of the

42. Coventry cathedral was bombed in an air raid. John Piper, one of the artists commissioned by the government to record the war, painted its ruins in 1940 (*above*), and later the stained glass windows of the reborn cathedral of 1955.

great names in British art: of Graham Sutherland, John Piper,
Francis Bacon, all of whom painted and drew the effect of war on
England.

Graham Sutherland and John Piper had a romantic, metaphysical view of nature: the bombed sites of cities suited the
dramatic bent in their styles very well, and both produced
haunted, almost phantasmagoric pictures of war damage. Piper's
ruined churches (see plate 42) far transcended their documentary
content; Sutherland drew on the immense riches of Christian
imagery to lament the violence and devastation of war. Paul Nash,
who had just been a War Artist in the trenches, became a Surrealist in the intervening years. This vision – of the nightmares of
the mind – created potent metamorphoses of the phenomena of
battle. His *Totes Meer* (see plate 43) – Dead Sea – is one of the
most memorable elegies of the Second World War. The huge
canvas depicts the carcasses of aeroplanes, wrecked one against
the other, their broken wings heaving, like white horses under

43. *Totes Meer* – Dead Sea. Paul Nash's surrealist painting transmutes the wreck-
age of bomber planes into a dream image. Nash was present as an artist in both
wars.

wind, while a pale, cold moon rises overhead. Edward Burra who had also painted during the First World War, though unlike Nash he had not been an official War Artist, gave free rein to his grotesque imagination during the Second World War, and captured the painful pleasure-seeking of soldiers on leave, the desperation of bars and pubs, the rowdiness of men 'having a good time'. He was always a painter of low-life and its splendours and its miseries: the War conferred legitimacy on his subject matter, and, again, brought him in communication with a much broader audience than ever before.

The Blitz created a feeling of solidarity among civilians; it helped to break down the class barriers, for mass evacuations of children took place, a manoeuvre that acquainted both halves of the population briefly with the way the other half lived – and behaved. Children from the industrial tenements of Manchester and the East End of London were billeted on landowners and country vicars who had never been exposed – as people are today through television – to the toughness of street life, and survival. Evelyn Waugh followed up his dazzling début (he was 25 when *Decline and Fall* was published) with other fun – *Vile Bodies, Black Mischief, Scoop* – at the expense of both his friends and his own aspirations. He recognized the fatal snobbery which made him hanker to live the life he vividly saw to be both hollow and cruel. In his first war novel, *Put Out More Flags* (1942), written on a troopship travelling to the war in West Africa, Evelyn Waugh uses his incomparable gift for black humour to describe the experiences of country gentry in the hands of the Connollys, a threesome of wild evacuee children who systematically wreck every house in which they are billeted. Waugh's hero, Basil Seal, discovers he can make money out of the Connollys, by accepting bribes to remove them. All over the country, discreet gentlefolk who have never stooped to crime, however petty, press money into Basil's hands to get rid of the Connollys.

Of course, Waugh's picture of evacuation is exaggerated: but, as always, his satire becomes hilarious because it is so very nearly exactly what happened.

In May, 1941, the Germans called off their attempt to prepare for a land invasion of England by defeating her first from the air, and concentrated their forces on defending the long exposed frontier with Russia, who had now come into the war on the Allies' side. The Blitz thus came to an end, though the air-raids and the blackout continued. And with the end of the Blitz came a temporary decline of those fellow-feelings that had sharpened men's courage and poets' inspiration. The novelist, Elizabeth Bowen, a subtle, mannered portraitist of social mores and powerful but contained emotions, wrote that 'war moved from the horizon to the map'. It became a distant phenomenon – and, as in the First World War, news was sketchy because censorship rendered information so cloudy that the people at home could not even keep track of the progress of the fighting.

This was possibly all to the good, as 1941 brought a series of crushing defeats for the Allies, and the death toll mounted sharply. In June, Hitler attacked Russia; in December the Japanese bombed Pearl Harbor, an American naval base in the Pacific, and thus brought America into the war. The defeat of Italy earlier in Libya and Abyssinia did not undo the mounting spectre of victory for the Axis powers – Germany and her satellites. One of the chief problems for England was armaments, and Churchill swung the country into a prodigious arms effort to gain mastery of the air and the sea. This was then supported by massive U.S. involvement. In 1940, the state of the force had been parlous. Anthony Powell, a contemporary of Evelyn Waugh's who has chronicled the society of his times in a long, humorous, gossipy sequence of twelve novels called *A Dance to the Music of Time*, the first volume of which was published in 1951, used a single main character, his narrator and alter ego Nicholas Jenkins, to follow the course of the war. The beginning finds him in training in a comical platoon composed of middle-aged professional men for officers, and Welsh miners for other ranks. Jenkins rests during an exercise, and contemplates the air power in the sky above him:

> When Macfaddean was gone, we found a place to lie under some
> withered trees, blasted, no doubt, to their crumbling state by frequent
> military experiment. We were operating over the dismal tundra of

Laffan's Plain, battlefield of a million mock engagements. The sky above was filled with low-flying aircraft, of outlandish colour and design, camouflaged perhaps by Barnby (*another character, a painter*) in a playful mood. Lumbering army reconnaissance planes buzzed placidly backwards and forwards through grey puffs of cloud, ancient machines garnered in from goodness knows what forgotten repository of written-off Government stores, now sent aloft again to meet a desperate situation. The heavens looked like one of those pictures of an imagined Future to be found in old-fashioned magazines for boys. . . .

Powell is enormously admired, for what is considered by some to be a Proustian grasp of social nuances and ironies, but his sensibility has little of the Frenchman's depths, and his humour, very sophisticated, urbane and charming, is none the less eclipsed by Waugh's brilliantly savage style.

This almost comical state of air power in 1939–40, as described by Powell, was redressed by the herculean efforts of the munition and aircraft workers. By the end of the Battle of Britain, the intrepid defence against German air attacks carried out by fighter pilots throughout 1940–41, the airforce had become a legend in its own time. This was largely due to the heroism of the flyers, who duelled in the skies like warriors in some mythological ancient epic, taking on German bombers in what amounted to hand-to-hand combat in the air. The pilot who was transformed into the Sir Gawain of this saga was Richard Hillary, who flew a Spitfire with immense daring until he was shot down in the Battle of Britain, and like many others, burned alive. He survived the horror, but his face and hands were disfigured. His intense account of his experience, *The Last Enemy*, was published in 1942. In it he described the nonchalant, arrogant way he had begun. He had joined up as one of the 'long-haired boys' in the Oxford University Air Squadron. But later his acquaintance with fighting, with love, and with the suffering and pity of a bomb victim he helped dig out after he was grounded, healed him of his casualness and made him see the deeper and more terrible implications of War. Hillary gained enormous fame after his book was published, and the pressure of becoming a living myth drove him back to seek oblivion as a pilot once again. He overcame the handicap of his burns, and began flying. He was killed, not by enemy action but in an accident, in January, 1943.

Hillary's personal document is one of the few cries from the heart produced by the Second World War. No soldier poet reached the intensity of Wilfred Owen; no forces' piece of prose the complexity and value of Robert Graves' *Goodbye to All That*. Among the men fighting, the war inspired a much more tolerant, uncommitted type of writing. Its far-flung character did not distil the pity of war in the way Wilfred Owen had required.

After the entry of Japan and America, the Second World War involved North Africa, the Middle East, the Sudan and Abyssinia, the whole of China and the Malay peninsula and even New Guinea as well as Europe, Western Russia and parts of Scandinavia. It was, in a way the First World War had not been, a true world war. It affected the lives of millions of people, military and civilian. For England, the decisive moment, when defeat was averted and victory seemed on the way, took place in the North African desert, when the battle of El Alamein routed Rommel's hitherto unbeatable Afrika Corps, and General Montgomery's Eighth Army found itself in command of North Africa, poised to start the invasion of Sicily and Italy. Such great battles of the Second World War have not made much mark in English literature – at least not yet.

Short stories and poems were preferred media for the contemporary witnesses, partly because the acute paper shortage at home meant that the publication of longer books was severely rationed. At the same time, the appetite of the public for reading matter became – for once – insatiable. The blackout, long periods of waiting at domestic wartime duties like firewatching or the Home Guard, the dearth of entertainment and the difficulties about going out at all meant that people had plenty of time to themselves. Anthologies of poetry, and of short stories, enjoyed an unprecedented popularity.

In 1944, Jonathan Cape published one of the few anthologies ever to become a best-seller – the favourite poetry of Field

Marshal Viscount Wavell, called *Other Men's Flowers*. The poet, Alun Lewis, also achieved fame during the war, with some terse, acutely perceived vignettes of the Far Eastern war in India and Burma. His scenes of army life, of its excitements and its pathos, have grandeur on a miniature scale and a vivid human dimension. But he did not tackle the larger questions, and his opus, cut short by his probable suicide while still out in the East, has left him with minor status.

The poet and writer with the highest claim to greatness during the Second World War is also the chief witness to the experience of the great victory of Alamein – Keith Douglas (see plate 44). He grasped the huge implications of the struggle, and was able, through a plain, strong style, to particularize it in his own circumstances. He was twenty when he joined up, as a junior officer in a

44. Keith Douglas, drawn here by himself, identified strongly with the poets of the First World War, and wrote with similar uncompromising honesty about the battles he fought on the African front in 1942–3.

tank regiment, and he fought in a Crusader tank up the desert
during the epic time of England's change of fortunes – from
October, 1942 to May, 1943, when Rommel was chased across
North Africa and surrendered. His account, *From Alamein to
Zem-Zem*, is illustrated by his own scribbled, but evocative water-
colours, and the text has a first-hand authenticity both rousing
and moving. His observation is at times poetically acute, although
in general, in his prose work, he tried to avoid anything but firm
simplicity:

> The view from a moving tank is like that in a camera obscura or a
> silent film – in that since the engine drowns all other voices except
> explosions, the whole world moves silently. Men shout, vehicles
> move, aeroplanes fly over, and all soundlessly: the noise of the tank
> being continuous, perhaps for hours on end, the effect is of silence . . .
> Silence is a strange thing to us who live: we desire it, we fear it, we
> worship it, we hate it. There is a divinity about cats, as long as they
> are silent: the silence of swans gives them an air of legend. The most
> impressive thing about the dead is their triumphant silence, proof
> against anything in the world.

Douglas' poetry delves into the lurid, violent images that Isaac
Rosenberg, one of his models, sought out to express the horrors
of the First World War. Douglas can also be very compressed,
very immediate. 'How to Kill' is a powerful, chilly, precise poem
about exactly that:

> Now in my dial of glass appears
>   the soldier who is going to die.
> He smiles, and moves about in ways
>   his mother knows, habits of his.
> The wires touch his face: I cry
>   NOW. Death, like a familiar, hears
> and look, has made a man of dust
>   of a man of flesh. This sorcery
> I do. Being damned, I am amused
>   to see the centre of love diffused
> and the waves of love travel into vacancy.
>   How easy it is to make a ghost.

Douglas returned to England with his regiment to prepare for the liberation of France, and was killed in Normandy, three days after D-Day, on 9th June, 1944. He was twenty-four, but even his youth and his bravery could not help to give him altogether the stature of Wilfred Owen.

Artists seem to work better as adversaries than supporters, and the bitterness of feelings about the First World War's futility was a spur to art in a way patriotism can never be. The cause of the Second World War was just; the art suffered from obedience to the strictures and limitations justifiably imposed by the Government on self-expression. Artists of the Second World War in England were not, by and large, in rebellion against its aims. In some areas, the acceptance of war's demands had damaged men's life's work. Musicians suffered from even less patronage than writers, and lack of employment could be chronic in wartime. William Walton wrote incidental music on commission for the BBC, but until he wrote the score for the patriotic, almost jingoistic version of *Henry V* with Laurence Olivier (see plate 49), made in 1944, he was unable to give himself to any long or serious undertaking.

The D-Day landings on the beaches of Normandy followed logically in the victorious phase of the European war that began with the recapture of North Africa and the conquest of Italy in 1943. The attacks ended at last the hideous indiscriminate aerial bombardments of German cities British Bomber Command had carried out, in a campaign that had lasted more than two years but had failed to wipe out German production and industry as intended. The D-Day landings began the Second Front offensive, involving the immense forces – armies of three and a half million Allies, British and American, that eventually liberated France and Belgium. With D-Day, total victory against Germany suddenly seemed a possibility, and the summer of 1944 saw English people enjoying themselves as best they could once again, in hope for a German surrender. On 8th May, 1945, after Churchill, Stalin and President Roosevelt had met to decide the future demarcation of power in Europe, Germany surrendered. The war in the Far East against Japan continued; it was ended by the explosion of the first atomic bomb at Hiroshima, on 6th August, and of the second at Nagasaki on 9th August. These weapons were used with almost no understanding of their consequences – neither on the immediate victims, nor for the world afterwards.

The death toll of the Second World War exceeds the first to an unimaginable degree. There are the incalculable number of victims of fall-out in Japan. There is the extermination of millions of Jews in Germany, Poland and other German-occupied countries. On the Russian Front 21,300,000 Russians were killed; in China 13½ million Chinese died in their struggle against Japan. In France, 360,000 civilians died; in Japan, the same number of civilians and 1,700,000 military men. German forces lost 3,250,000; the British and Commonwealth figure, 452,000, was much lower. It was a holocaust: in all, including the Jews who died in the concentration camps, over 55 million people died.

The British people suffered terrible hardships at home; 60,000 civilians died. For them, the peace meant a new era. The Second World War had, like the First, allowed the winds of revolution to blow in the most stately and sedate corridors of Whitehall. As early as November, 1942, William Beveridge, a civil servant, drew up a blueprint, in his famous Beveridge Report, for a new country, a country where the pre-war epidemic of Want, Disease, Ignorance, Squalor and Idleness would be contained, and state measures to protect the poor and needy and improve the lot of all would be passed. The experience of war made men suffer almost equally; it had given them the habit of central collective planning. War had exhausted the value of the old society and made it search for new ideas. In the first General Election following peace, Churchill, the 'Saviour of his country' was turned aside, and the Labour leader, Clement Attlee, asked to form a cabinet to lead the country. The first post-war government was to be innovative, progressive; it created the welfare state in the form in which it is still recognizable today in Britain, and which still constitutes a remarkable social experiment in mutual care and concern. It was not, however, a peculiarly Socialist creation, for its guidelines had been laid down in some detail by Beveridge, who was a Liberal himself, and working then for the National

Government under Churchill. War made the welfare state necessary and acceptable to all, socialists and non-socialists alike. It helped to alter England in a way that had been urgent since before the First World War; yet people were still surprised at the promised changes. As one of the soldiers in *'Ward "O" 3 (b)'*, a short story by Alun Lewis comments on the Beveridge Report:

> 'I don't want to go back "home",' Brownlow-Grace said, laying sardonic stress on the last word.
> 'I don't know,' Dad said. 'They tell me it's a good country to get into, this 'ere England. Why, I was only reading in the Bombay Times this morning there's a man Beaverage (sic) or something, made a report, they even give you money to bury yourself with there now. Suits me.' 'You won't die, Dad,' Brownlow-Grace said kindly. 'You'll simply fade away.'

㊉㊉㊉㊉㊉

PAIN AND PLENTY

㊉㊉㊉㊉㊉

When first I heard that story it seemed incredible
That one betrayed;
But now, having lived my own, more wonderful
That eleven stayed
Even so precariously, so stupidly, so tentatively faithful
So few are true; and I,
In others as in myself despising him who died,
Not once but many times have done what Judas did,
Yet sorrowed less than he,
For I still live, not hang on any purple blossoming tree.

KATHLEEN RAINE *Judas Tree*

VICTORY is better than defeat; of that there can be no doubt when the enemy was Hitler's regime. But victory does not mean hegemony, wealth, solutions. The end of the war found the English people with empty pockets and empty larders, because six years of unremitting labour and fight had plunged Britain into enormous debt. In 1947, America, seeing the economic plight of her allies in Europe, organized an immense loan called the Marshall Plan, in order to rebuild the countries that had most suffered the devastation of war. With this financial help supporting the energy and courage that came with victory, the British people set about consolidating their pioneer state where the individual would be cared for.

The Labour Government, under the mild and high-principled Prime Minister, Clement Attlee (see plate 45), introduced immediately the notable economic reforms that had long been mooted and which were to transform the structure of human relationships

45. Clement Attlee was Britain's first Labour Prime Minister after the Second World War. His combination of probity and effectiveness made possible the great post-war Socialist reforms.

in English society. The nationalization of the Health Service became effective in 1948, when the private voluntary hospitals were taken over and incorporated into a national medical system providing attention for everyone – free. In this respect Britain was a pathfinder: many other European countries have since emulated the National Health Service's idealism, but it still remains an exceptional experiment. The United States, for instance, does not have a public medical service, but requires expensive private insurance from every individual before doctors will perform their art.

Other essential services were also taken over by the Government: the mines passed into public control in 1947, the Bank of England the year before, and electricity, gas and the railways in 1948.

Council homes, which constituted only 1 per cent of all housing in 1911, began rising in number and have now reached 30 per cent of the existing stock of houses. Enormous investments by the state in social services began. The National Insurance Act of 1946 made it mandatory for the state to protect the unemployed, the old, and others in special circumstances – handicap, pregnancy, chronic illness, in return for compulsory contributions levelled on the working individual. Education was reorganized: the youthful slavery of school leavers entering apprenticeships as Kipps had done was postponed for one year when the law was changed to extend schooling to 15-year olds. The 11-plus exam was introduced at the time, as a progressive measure, designed to encourage the able and to take better care of the less able by dividing them into different schools. The grammar schools concentrated on intellectual achievements; the secondary moderns provided more technical and manual training for the older children. This division has now been discredited as anti-democratic and unfair. Specialists in education came to realize that the labelling of children at eleven was both unreasonable and inaccurate, so the more flexible Comprehensive System was developed, the first school being opened in 1954 (see plate 46). The intention now is that all children, of whatever degree of aptitude, should be taught together, in order to avoid deepening the enduring class and ability structure in England. All in all, in the new British state, the indigent, the out-of-work and the sick would no longer feel the terror of need, the deprived would be assisted, and education would be available to all.

Clement Attlee was a singular politician: unassuming, disinterested, and both eager and able to appoint brilliant men to help him. His team won the public's heart after the war by inspiring the same kind of loyalty to England that Churchill, more pugnaciously, had done in wartime: they excited a sense of togetherness, of community, while their planned society seemed to hold out hopes for the extinction of the class conflict that had fractured pre-war life.

After a settled five years, Labour won another General Election, but the party was bedevilled by illness and death, and was

46. This comprehensive school in Pimlico, London, was purpose-built with a good
use of imagination by state-employed architects in 1970.

losing many of the great men who had made it what it was. In
1951, Churchill was returned as leader of the country, at the head
of a Conservative Government. It was a postponed acknowledgement of his quasi-papal status in English life. In 1955, aged 80, he
retired in favour of Sir Anthony Eden. Eden misjudged the post-
war climate and took a belligerent stand when Colonel Nasser,
Egypt's Nationalist leader, announced that Egypt was about to
nationalize the Suez Canal, a vital route for British trade. Eden
ordered troops into Egypt, but the intervention was a humiliating
failure and brought scorn upon Eden's head at home and abroad.
The last extravagant gesture of British imperialism finished his
career. He resigned to give way for Harold Macmillan. Suave,
highly effective, charming and very able, Macmillan was the
Prime Minister who presided over Britain's years of plenty. The
Affluent Society flourished in his day, and he summed up its
atmosphere with the catch phrase of his premiership 'You've

never had it so good'. The workers replied in kind. 'I'm all right, Jack' was the cheerful slogan of Britain's brief moment of confident prosperity.

But if the post-war experience of Britain has had a unifying theme, it is the realization of the incapacity of the state to solve human problems. This is not to say the welfare state, so bravely pioneered by Britain, has not been an extraordinary and admirable enterprise, but that the alchemy of a successful society demands ingredients that are not material only. Nothing can be achieved without money, but many things cannot be obtained with it. The fortunes of Florence in the late fifteenth century were necessary to the flowering of humanist values and the art they inspired. But prosperity is never a sufficient cause. The situation and the quality of life in England has undoubtedly improved for most people since 1900, but not for the rich at the very top end, nor for the poor at the very bottom. The broad band of the middle have benefited the most materially; but culturally there has been no flowering of poetry or of painting or of novel-writing comparable, say, to the fertility of England's imagination in the reign of Elizabeth I or of Queen Victoria. A certain quality of glory in self, or of faith, or of dynamism is lacking. And the inadequacies of the great experiment in social planning must share in the blame.

The old problems linking poverty with distress still persist stubbornly. The National Health has performed wonders: infant mortality has fallen, the near-sighted are given glasses, the toothless dentures, the crippled chairs, sticks or even cars at subsidized prices. The country paid £3,922 million in 1974 to maintain the Health Service, yet the basic state of the community's health has not improved greatly. It was thought, in the Forties, that improved care would lower the amount of illness, that preventive medicine would create a healthier people with a lower medical bill on the State. This has proved a pipe-dream, and the National Health service can hardly keep up with the demands of the community. An arthritic victim can wait months for the hip operation that will make the difference between agony and normality; the same for sufferers from kidney disease. Before, of course, there would have been no treatment at all.

This comparative failure colours the experiment of the post-war years in every area. Nothing has been an unqualified success. In housing the struggle has been particularly fierce: millions have been spent on building houses, in planning estates, on even constructing new towns. But forecasts have often turned out badly wrong: the high rise flats of the Sixties' housing explosion in London have empty upper storeys because people dislike living in them so much; a New Town, like Harlow, with every amenity thought out beforehand, has withered from its inception. Subsidized rent acts and other laws, protecting tenants of all kinds, have been passed. Yet the number of homeless grows, in spite of these efforts. In 1974, it stood at 28,546; compared to 5,825 in 1950. The problem of overcrowding has been whittled down, however: less than 2 per cent now live 2 to a room or more. In 1911, 9 per cent of the population did. But a house could be bought outright in the 1900s or after the First World War for a smaller sum in ratio to a worker's earnings than today, when a home can cost a family nearly three times the breadwinner's yearly wage and therefore hold a family in debt, sometimes as long as their working lifetime.

Travel, too, inside Britain, has become less available to the less well off. An enormous grid of roads, many of them motorways since the first was built in 1958, now covers the landscape; trains were severely cut back in 1963 when the Beeching Report decreed the closure of hundreds of branch lines. British Rail continues to lose money, and the motorways, though efficient, have disfigured the countryside. But internal travel is expensive: rail fares rise with astonishing steepness yearly. The prices of tickets on public transport within cities are increased regularly and flagrantly. But cars, the alternative method, are also very expensive indeed and cost more now both to buy and to run in relation to earnings than they did in the early years of the first family car, the Ford Model T.

Yet, of course, many more people have cars now than ever before; and travel abroad, a luxury known only to the rich in the 1900s, is now commonplace for summer holidays. Indeed, the guaranteed paid holiday for a working man was an exceptional privilege existing in few jobs right through the Thirties. So there have been some major improvements in the quality of life.

The contrast between prosperity and reform on the one hand, and futility and aridity on the other is reflected very accurately in the culture of post-war Britain. For the last 20 years, the British mind has been split over the issue of mass art (see colour plate 8). It has been the age when more people have been able to read more books, watch more plays, films, television documentaries and shows, look at more pictures and sculpture, listen to more music than ever before. There are over 18 million television sets in England; in 1967, colour was introduced, creating a magic realism on the small screen and greatly expanding the medium's accuracy and fidelity to such things as sports reports, especially those covering racing, football and tennis. 36,322 books were published in 1977, of which 27,284 were new titles. Books have become an industry, and a source of income for the country.

Orchestras have gone from strength to strength; the BBC is patron of several, some based in the provinces, all with notable reputations. The Royal Festival Hall was built in 1951; later the imposing South Bank complex of two concert halls, the National Film Theatre and the Hayward Gallery, an enormous space designed to house visiting exhibitions, was built next to it. It was designed by Sir Denys Lasdun and it commands a vista of the Thames and the Houses of Parliament, thus constituting an attempt to open London's gaze on the artery of its river, as most of the beautiful cities of the world, Paris, Budapest, Prague, have always done. English music has had a renaissance. The Edinburgh Festival, begun in 1947, has consistently sponsored or inspired new work or high standard renderings of old masterpieces both in the theatre and in music. The Aldeburgh Festival (see plate 47), started by the composer of genius, Benjamin Britten, in his beloved Suffolk, has also invited work and performances of an astonishingly high order since 1948, and the tradition has taken root so firmly that not even the composer's death in 1977 could shake it. Britten expanded the English tradition of intense and simple lyricism, founded on a complex and experimental use of musical techniques and an innovatory use of the human voice as

47. The Maltings, at Snape, was a brewery until Benjamin Britten converted it into the Aldeburgh Festival's principal concert hall.

the most eloquent instrument of all that is first found in the earlier masters of this century's music, like Vaughan Williams and Delius. Britten wrote beautiful works that explore the voice's subtlety and range: operas like *Peter Grimes* and *Billy Budd*, song cycles like the settings of poems by John Donne or Arthur Rimbaud, and his great oratorio, 'The War Requiem', a passionate, chaste lament for man's urge to destroy that uses the poetry of Wilfred Owen and the Mass for the Dead together. One of the great English performers who form part of the Renaissance of singing in this century is Peter Pears, Britten's life-long companion and his greatest interpreter. The long rich and varied opus of Britten has given British music a proud sense of identity, which is being expanded and strengthened all the time, by his contemporaries – Lennox Berkeley, Elizabeth Maconchy, Michael Tippett – and by younger musicians – John Taverner, Peter Maxwell Davies – who extend Britten's preoccupation with religious imagery and the possibilities of language in music.

In 1976 the National Theatre (see plate 48), beside the Festival Hall on the river, and also designed by Sir Denys Lasdun, was opened. Raised at a cost to the State of about £17 million, it proclaims the continuing faith of British governments in the necessity of the arts. The brutalist architecture of blank concrete

48. The magnificent and spacious National Theatre, built on London's South Bank, represents the apogee of the post-war policy of state subsidy for the arts.

expanses in ziggurat-like formation over the river has been fiercely criticized, as has the cost of the building and its upkeep. But it provides three auditoriums, scope for new British playwriting, and above all, a venue for one of the strongest British talents to emerge since the war: theatre production.

In direction, design and performance Britain has proved abundant talent throughout the post-war period. Cecil Beaton, a stylish portrait photographer, is also a designer of delightful, extravagant imagination. His costumes for *My Fair Lady* (1956) were a masterpiece. The numbers of actors and actresses who have taken the art into a realm of both pleasure and seriousness are far too great in number to describe. Laurence Olivier (see plate 49) works himself into a part, altering his appearance completely with make-up, voice change, a different gait. Most famous for his Shakespearean roles (Henry V, Othello, Coriolanus) he has worked interestingly in dozens of films, both in England and

49. Laurence Olivier played Shakespeare's Henry V in a famous early effort of the British film industry, made during the war to rally Britain's fighting spirit.

abroad, and so his consummate ability has reached a wider public than the ticket-buying theatre audience. Unlike his predecessors in fame on the English stage, Garrick or Irving, his face is known to everyone – almost.

In spite of the spread of the arts and the liveliness of interest, the divide between high culture and low culture has never been sharper: the theatre mainly survives in the provinces through state subsidy, while the British film industry, never truly flourishing, has almost ceased to exist. Television keeps people in their homes. The question for its programme controllers, who are ultimately responsible to a government body for their decisions, is how to balance material for which there is an enormous public demand with material of interest to few. It is disappointing that television's greatest successes have not created new forms or expressed new ideas: series like 'The Forsyte Saga' (see plate 50) or 'Upstairs Downstairs' 'or 'Days of Hope' play on audiences' appetite for nostalgia and retrospection. They build little new.

50. Susan Hampshire and Eric Porter in the television adaptation of Galsworthy's
The Forsyte Saga. The Edwardian age has recently become the subject of popular
nostalgia.

Radio since the war has sponsored some adventurous work – more
so than television. The Welsh poet Dylan Thomas, whose work is
a parade of glittering images, wrote his masterpiece, *Under Milk
Wood*, for the BBC in 1953. Written for several voices, it is a
tender-hearted evocation of a village and its characters, with their
peculiarities and their hates and their loves.

One of the reasons for the unpopularity of so-called high art is
that its subject matter is depressing. There is no doubt the post-
war period has seen the intensification of the gloom that characterizes influential twentieth-century art. This is the time of the
bomb, of the spread of dictatorships and torture, of forces of
destruction unleashed against innocent people, of the collapse of
the rich societies of the west. Such ideas are not cheerful, they are
painful to hear, and impossible to solve. Therefore, the larger
audiences gravitate to escapist culture, and in spite of huge
resources deployed to foster it, art is still the domain of a small

51. Samuel Beckett's *Waiting for Godot*, here photographed in the first London production of 1955, was probably the most unpredictable wild success of the century.

élite, and its predominant theme is despair. Man's immense powers for self-destruction are contrasted to the littleness of his spiritual capacities; the accessibility of riches and power is compared to the emotional emptiness of the individual; the vast organized fabric of society is shown to engulf the people within it. But futility and the sense of meaninglessness have penetrated all modern European literature so deeply that the case cannot be said to be peculiarly British. It certainly belongs to Britain, too, though, for some of the most articulate voices of contemporary goallessness have come from Britain.

Samuel Beckett, born in Ireland, of Protestant extraction, has become a dominant voice of the twentieth century: he apprehends the comic in cosmic emptiness, and expresses it through tramps, through clowns, through derelicts and vagabonds, who are always the heroes and heroines of his novels – *Molloy, Malone Dies* – and of his more famous plays, *Endgame, Happy Days*, and the most celebrated of all – *Waiting for Godot* (see plate 51). First performed in 1953, in Paris, Beckett's adoptive town, *Waiting for Godot* has become the metaphor for our age. The tramps joke, philosophize, bicker, reminisce on stage for over two hours while awaiting the arrival of Godot. It is never said exactly who Godot is, what he will do, what they expect of him; and, of course, he never comes. It is a play about whiling away life at one level, about degree zero of the soul at another. It is technically masterly, unceasingly interesting, and exhibits Beckett's instinctive understanding of the craft of acting, and also, more particularly, of clowning. Yet afterwards, it is difficult to know what was said and impossible to know what was meant by it. The dialogue is pared down, yet aimless, concrete yet elusive:

ESTRAGON: I tell you I wasn't doing anything.
VLADIMIR: Perhaps you weren't. But it's the way of doing it that counts, the way of doing it, if you want to go on living.
ESTRAGON: I wasn't doing anything.
VLADIMIR: You must be happy too, deep down, if you only knew it.
ESTRAGON: Happy about what?
VLADIMIR: To be back with me again.
ESTRAGON: Would you say so?
VLADIMIR: Say you are, even if it's not true.
ESTRAGON: What am I to say?
VLADIMIR: Say, I am happy.
ESTRAGON: I am happy.
VLADIMIR: So am I.
ESTRAGON: So am I.
VLADIMIR: We are happy.
ESTRAGON: We are happy. (*Silence*) What do we do now, now that we are happy?
VLADIMIR: Wait for Godot.

Other master dramatists have exploded with rage at twentieth-century man's sensation of powerlessness. John Osborne in *Look Back in Anger* (see plate 52) caused an excited controversy with his dramatic and violent portrait of Jimmy Porter, the prototype of the Angry Young Man, filled with talent, with energy,

52. A scene from the film of John Osborne's play *Look Back in Anger*, with Richard Burton and Mary Ure. It expressed the frustration of the 'Angry Young Men's' generation, and sparked a revival of the English playwriting tradition.

with ideas, and finding himself frustrated at every turn by the conventions and the narrowness of the company he keeps. Arnold Wesker broadened the vision of modern man by dramatizing social settings and the toll they take on human sensibilities. In *The Kitchen*, his protagonist, labouring under the stress of fast food catering in hellish circumstances, eventually goes berserk.

Harold Pinter, another living playwright, forsook the traditional context of social realism and instead created an elliptical, almost abstract world in which the spectators' attention is focused on points of highwire tension between his characters, caused not by great upheavals but by small explosions of emotion and by the perpetual quest of one person to dominate another.

The proclamation of life's meaninglessness and sufferings is also made by other artists in every medium. Philip Larkin, one of England's clearest living poets, writes black elegies on the modern condition, and sees no reprieve. A famous lyric, 'This Be The Verse', hands out this harsh advice:

Man hands on misery to man.
It deepens like a coastal shelf.
Get out as early as you can,
And don't have any kids yourself.

Even the tradition of nature poetry, coming down through the passion of Shakespeare's observation to the effusions of Wordsworth and the voluptuousness of Keats, gains a dimension of cruelty and sorrow in the hands of its greatest contemporary master, Ted Hughes. His *alter ego*, Crow, becomes a symbol of genesis, the dark, unformed beginning of all life. But that life is predatory, doomed to death, and full of pain. One litany expresses very well Hughes' feeling for the naked savagery of all creation. It reveals his response to the hard Anglo-Saxon backbone of the English language, as well as his naturalist's eye.

In the beginning was Scream
Who begat Blood
Who begat Eye
Who begat Fear
Who begat Wing
Who begat Bone
Who begat Granite
Who begat Violet
Who begat Guitar
Who begat Sweat
Who begat Adam
Who begat Mary
Who begat God
Who begat Nothing
Who begat Never
Never, Never Never

Who begat Crow

Screaming for Blood
Grubs, crusts
Anything
Trembling featherless elbows in the nest's filth.

Hughes was married to the American poet, Sylvia Plath, who has now, after her suicide in 1963, become the focus of a fervent cult. She wrote her great poetry in England, during her marriage, and it displays a unique sensibility, feeling out the quick of emotion and creating an atmosphere of restrained violence. Hers is a continual fight against the sense of the void, for she is always trying, through pain or even illness, to feel alive:

> Dying is an art, like everything else.
> I do it exceptionally well.
> I do it so it feels like hell.
> I do it so it feels real.

Resignation to emptiness turns into protest, but not action. The sigh is not enough; the scream gets nearer the feel of it. The greatest painter of contemporary nihilism is Francis Bacon. He takes the most ancient image of salvation, the Crucifixion, and nails down all its horror, seeing the body of Christ as a worm crawling down the cross (see colour plate 9). He has painted a series of variations on Velasquez's famous portraits of Renaissance Popes; but the acute, detailed faces of the Old Master become blurred phantasms, leering, decaying images from the deep. He uses paint as if it were slime, and applies it smudgily, streakily but always with exceptional expressiveness, so that his people always seem to be returning to the primaeval chaos, to formlessness, to indeterminateness. Bacon has said, 'I think that man now realizes that he is an accident, that he is a completely futile being, that he has to play out the game without reason.' So Bacon paints the howl of modern humanity, trying to capture it alive on canvas. He has also said that painting 'is something to do with instinct. It's a very very close and difficult thing to know why some paint comes across directly on to the nervous system and other paint tells you the story in a long diatribe through the brain.'

In that comment, on the method of creation at which he aims, Bacon expresses a central theme in post-war art: that the artist should absorb feelings, not ideas, transform them within his psyche, and recommunicate them to his audience, as intelligible emotion. Ideas, didacticism, intellect, history, description, landscape, social mores no longer count as the main matter of art. Art is psychology, it charts the soul.

Bacon has no school; his influence is psychological, not stylistic. One of the other great living painters in England, Lucien Freud (see colour plate 10), shares much in common with Bacon's sensibility, though his art has a different appearance, being almost surrealistically accurate in its attention to the detail of physiognomy and anatomy. His fascination with flesh is cold, and almost nauseated. He seems to be painting out of deep disgust mingled with pity, but the kind of pity that can hardly bear to look on the pitiable creature or object, so degraded is it.

These two represent the mainstream of the modernist tradition in English figurative art. The most famous younger contemporary painter, David Hockney (see colour plate 11), has inherited little of their pain, a factor which might account in part for his enormous public. He is not a difficult painter. His paintings are not hard to live with. They are controlled, unemotional, descriptive and often witty. Even when he disturbs, he does not despair. He is also an inspired illustrator using etching technique with finesse.

There have also been figurative artists in England who have created their own cosmos without relation, it appears, to the circumstances of the day: Stanley Spencer (died 1959) who all his life painted his visions of God and his saints and situated them in the fields and churchyard and lanes of his Thames valley village, Cookham. Jack Yeats, (d. 1957) brother of the poet, used paint exuberantly, squeezing bright colours directly out of the tube on to the canvas, expressing a private, hectic vitality (see colour plate 4). Beckett wrote of his 'incomparable hand shaken . . . by its own urgency.'

Another response to the complexity of modern life was abstraction, the severing of links between the objective world and the painter. The English non-figurative school has included some very fine artists, notably Ben Nicolson, whose chaste, precise geometry has an almost Oriental understanding of harmony. The sculptor, Barbara Hepworth (died 1975), worked with abstract shapes as well as figures (see plate 53), as does her mentor and

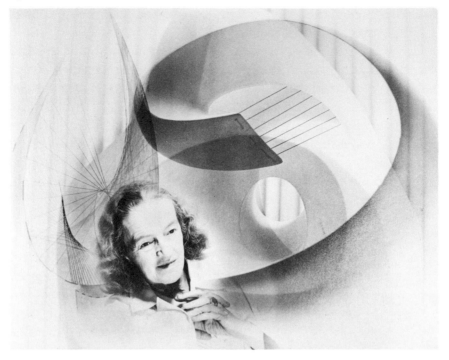

53. Barbara Hepworth, photographed here by Jorge Lewinski in a montage of her sculpture, was deeply concerned with the natural texture and colour of the wood or stone or metal she was using, and sought to represent the organic shapes of the Cornish landscape where she lived.

inspiration, Henry Moore. Fidelity to materials, the discovery of a stone's essential qualities of shape and grain and colour is one of the aims of this form of elemental sculpture. It bypasses comment on the human condition by emptying itself of all social or psychological content so that it almost reaches the condition of music. Moore, Hepworth and Nicolson are great figures in English art, but their abstract work reflects the internationalism of all culture in the world today; it is not a specific symptom of English life.

The English demonstrate their genius more often through close involvement with the issue of man in society. The novel has, for instance, been a form at which the English have long excelled. The post-war period has seen a flowering of social consciousness in this form. Henry Green has a pellucid, tender style of great elegance and depth and he uses it to catch the web of loyalty and love in which individuals struggle to be happy. His sequence of novels, amongst which *Loving* (1945) and *Party-Going* (1939) are the most famous, contain no censure and little sarcasm, and yet they express with cruel clarity the assumptions and the failings of the upper classes in Britain, and the deep divide that exists between this small minority and the rest of society. In *Loving*, a huge, empty country house in Ireland is the setting for the poignant courtship of a butler and a chambermaid during the Second World War. As Green unfolds the story, he creates lasting images: the game of blind man's buff in the hall where the statues are shrouded, the rubdown of one tired maid by another.

Another novelist of stature, Graham Greene, has a greater and more overt political consciousness. He interweaves astute political judgement, the feel of a thriller, and absorption with the human heart and conscience. Novels like *The Quiet American* (1955), set in Vietnam, *A Burnt-Out Case*, set in Mexico, *The Heart of the Matter*, set in West Africa, *The Comedians*, set in Haiti, *The Honorary Consul*, set in Mexico, dramatize painful moral dilemmas in exciting, fast flowing narratives against political backgrounds. Graham Greene became a Catholic in 1926, and his writing is steeped in a sense of irredeemable sin. Over a very long career (his first novel was published in the late Twenties) he has distinguished himself for a scrupulous, raw conscience that has excited the sympathy of an enormous international audience. For a fine artist, his is a very wide, popular following.

Other English novelists, like John Braine in *Room At The Top* (1957) have illustrated the flow of class prejudice and ambition that still persists in English society. Many women have spoken of the problem of sexual subordination and the stifling of female independence, notably the Southern Rhodesian, Doris Lessing, who has lived in London since 1949, a writer of depth, sympathy and redoubtable integrity. The tradition of British humour has not disappeared completely in the gloom. Kingsley Amis's *Lucky Jim* (1954) is still one of the funniest novels ever written.

The prevailing bleakness of atmosphere was alleviated at one time – briefly. London rose from the austerity of the Forties and Fifties to a zenith in the Sixties as the swinging capital, the entertainment and fashion centre of the world. Fashion designers like Mary Quant invented an off-beat image of the fun-loving, dashing, confident and progressive English girl; Carnaby Street, selling bright clothes, replied with her male equivalent, in floral tie and shirt; the Beatles swept the world with their abounding sense of joy in life.

> She loves you, yeah, yeah, yeah,
> She loves you, yeah, yeah, yeah,
> With a love like that
> You know you should be glad.

But the upswing was short; the Beatles themselves retreated into eccentricity, melancholy and soul-searching and eventually were destroyed as a group. Their high spirits were a marvellous expression of the times; so was their disintegration. Swinging London was index-linked to prosperity. When the economic boom of the Sixties ended, the disaffection quickly returned, and with it the shrinking pains that have beset England since the war.

The transition from a great empire to a commonwealth was achieved with remarkable ease and some harmony, but British citizens from commonwealth countries have experienced prejudice and tension here, which political parties of the right, notably the National Front and even some irresponsible members of the Conservatives, have exploited for their own ends. The popularity of the monarchy, and of the Queen herself, seems to have little power to alleviate these problems though she visits commonwealth countries regularly, and recognizes, by bestowing official honours on individual leaders, their contribution to the position of Britain in the world. Mahatma Gandhi, for instance, the pacifist leader of Indian nationalism, was first treated disgracefully by the British, harassed, and even imprisoned. But his wisdom, integrity and justice were at last recognized, and he is now honoured by a statue in Russell Square, Bloomsbury.

One of the worst prevalent contemporary attitudes is the ignorance shown, even by people who are not prejudiced, about the benefits Britain draws from the heterogeneousness of its society. Citizens who came originally from former colonies or dominions, from India, Pakistan, the West Indies, Africa, or from Hong Kong, which is still under British rule, have enriched the country, not only by their invaluable labour, but also by the different cultural and religious and philosophical and social attitudes with which they broaden and enliven English life. Insularity has been a British curse, xenophobia a national illness, and it is time for this to pass, and for it to be understood that a nation withers at its roots if it does not receive continual stimulus from outside influences. The Press, in race questions, is usually excitable.

An abiding problem, which makes such changes in attitudes difficult to achieve, is the quality of the country's leadership. Political life has suffered a steep decline in status. Harold Wilson, for instance, Labour's second Prime Minister since the war, proved as slippery as Lloyd George and far less able or inspired. He resigned, for reasons that are still not understood, in 1976, and his reputation remains tainted by self-seeking. But the chief source of disillusion has been the ever-fugitive vision of the successful and just society. Taxes rise, wages lose value, crime increases, poverty refuses to disappear. On the other hand, some causes, the rights of workers and the equality of women have made progress.

Progress has also been made, most significantly, in the attitudes to social inequality, not in the inequality itself. It is no longer acceptable behaviour to flaunt social divisions of class or wealth. But England remains a divided nation. The top 10 per cent who owned 92 per cent of the national capital in 1911–13 still own 83 per cent today. It is an astonishing figure. In education in parparticular little headway has been made against social disadvantage. In 1967, while school-leavers from public and direct grant schools constituted under 10 per cent of pupils at all schools in the country, they formed over 60 per cent of undergraduates at Oxbridge and over 30 per cent of all university students.

England is still looking for an identity, and its artists can only express that search and its painfulness. One of the finest novelists today, V. S. Naipaul, an Indian from the Caribbean, has caught the floundering of the contemporary English character very well in his powerful story of West Indian revolutionary politics,

Guerillas (1975). He describes an English girl who becomes involved with a man deported from South Africa:

> In London Roche had seemed to her an extraordinary person; and she had prided herself on her perception in picking him out. He had appeared to her as a doer; and none of the people she knew could be considered doers. They grumbled, journalists, politicians, business-men, responding week by week to the latest newspaper crisis and television issue; they echoed one another; they could become hysteri-cal with visions of the country's decay. But the little crises always passed, the whispered political plots and business schemes evapo-rated; everything that was said was stale, and people no longer believed what was said. And failure always lay with someone else: the people who spoke of the crisis were themselves placid, content with their functions, existing within their functions, trapped, part of what they railed against.
>
> She was adrift, enervated, her dissatisfaction vague, now centring on the world, now on men.

With this quick portrait of a single woman, Naipaul catches that enervation which affects so much of contemporary life in England today. Economic reasons seem to determine so much in such a baffling way that the individual feels dwarfed and helpless. At one level this leads to Punk Rock, dead end music; at another to the short play of Samuel Beckett, *Breath*, in which nothing at all happens. The rest is indeed silence.

Yet at both ends of today's culture – mandarin and exclusive or vernacular and inclusive – the sense of aimlessness is counter-balanced by something else, by something more positive. After all, the act of creation, of singing or performing or writing is in itself an affirmation of the human being's existence, and represents a substantial attempt to give shape to things through art. This is no paltry matter, and our contemporary British society, though it has not yet fostered the distinction of a Shakespeare or a Keats, probably sustains a greater number of people working in the arts than at any other time in the nation's history.

There is also a swelling undertow to the prevailing bleakness, a movement linked to the social and political developments since the war. With the acknowledgement of Britain's decline in power,

and with the growth all over the world, and especially in the
United States, of a greater awareness of mankind's responsibility
to nature and of the heavy toll industrial society has taken of
human values, there has come a feeling of humility and of
acceptance, that is neither particularly pessimistic nor optimistic,
but a quiet and gentle state, bringing with it an appreciation of
small scale endeavour, the private accomplishments of individuals.
Britain is no longer poised to conquer and command, to expand
and profit, to achieve and dominate. The canvas has shrunk, but
that does not mean it has less value or less significance. The state's
established concern for the individual is reflected in present day
culture's examination of daily life, and of the personal values of
each man and woman. It is a wide, wide-open vista, for neither
church nor state provides that cast iron moral code of yesterday.
This contemporary quest – for the right way to conduct a life –
illuminates much of today's writing and painting with a light that
is softer than the razzle-dazzle of the turn of the century's adventure stories, or the bright lamps of Wells' early social commen-
taries, that is more intimate and more commonplace than the
brilliant experiments of the Twenties, more glowing than the
fanatic gleams of the Thirties revolutionaries. It gives a sense of
each person's accountability in the here and now. This modern
viewpoint has been firmly and simply captured by Peter Porter,
an Australian-born poet who now lives in Britain. In a new collec
tion, *The Cost of Seriousness*, he writes as if his dead wife were
talking to him from the grave. She tells him what she has discovered, and in these few lines, epitomizes a growing impatience
with the irresponsibility of despair:

> There is no morality,
> no metered selfishness, or cowardly fear.
> What we do on earth is its own parade
> and cannot be redeemed in death. The pity
> of it, that we are misled. By mother,
> saying her sadness is the law, by love,
> hiding itself in evenings of ethics,
> by despair, turning the use of limbs
> to lockjaw.   The artist knows this.

And knowing it – or having recently learned it – must now try and say it. And in all the confusion and disappointments of modern life, such knowledge is hard to gain, harder still to speak.

ⓖⓖⓖⓖⓖ

BIBLIOGRAPHY

ⓖⓖⓖⓖⓖ

The literature of the century is so vast that I can only provide the barest outlines. Below I cite the books I have either consulted or quoted in the text: I hope they will lead the reader to explore much further. Similarly, the 'Fiction for the Same Age Group' list gives only a few suggestions taken from the wealth of material available.

I. BACKGROUND MATERIAL

Addison, Paul. *The Road to 1945: British Politics and the Second World War.* Quartet Books, London, 1977

Asquith, Lady Cynthia. *Diaries 1915–18.* Hutchinson, London, 1968

Branson, Noreen and Heinemann, Margot. *Britain in the Nineteen Thirties.* Panther, St Albans, 1973

Calder, Angus. *The People's War: Britain 1939–45.* Jonathan Cape, London, 1969

Dangerfield, George. *The Strange Death of Liberal England.* Panther (Paladin), St Albans, 1970

Hewison, Robert. *Under Siege: Literary Life in London 1939–45.* Weidenfeld and Nicolson, London, 1977

Keegan, John. *The Face of Battle.* Jonathan Cape, London, 1976

Lowndes, Marie Belloc. *Diaries and Letters 1917–47.* Edited by Susan Lowndes. Chatto and Windus, London, 1971

McElwee, William. *Britain's Locust Years, 1918–1940.* Faber, London, 1962

Mowat, Charles Loch. *Britain Between the Wars, 1918–1940.* Methuen, London, 1968

Stallworthy, Jon. *Wilfred Owen: A Biography.* Oxford University Press, London, 1974

Sylvester, David. *Interviews with Francis Bacon.* Thames and Hudson, London, 1975

Taylor, A. J. P. *English History 1914–1945.* Penguin, Harmondsworth, 1970

Thompson, Paul. *The Edwardians: The Remaking of British Society.* Panther (Paladin), St Albans, 1977

Thomson, David. *England in the Twentieth Century, 1914-1963*. Penguin (Pelican History of England), Harmondsworth, 1970
Williams, Raymond. *Culture and Society 1780-1950*. Penguin, Harmondsworth, 1971

2. LITERATURE OF THE TIME

Auden, W. H. *Collected Poems*. Faber, London, 1976
—— *Selected Poems*. Faber (paperback), London, 1968
Beckett, Samuel. *Waiting for Godot*. Faber, London, 1956
Conrad, Joseph. *The Secret Agent*. Penguin, Harmondsworth, 1969
Douglas, Keith. *From Alamein to Zem Zem*. Penguin, Harmondsworth, 1969
Eliot, T. S. *Collected Poems 1909-62*. Faber (paperback), London, 1974
Gardner, Brian (Ed.). *The Terrible Rain: The War Poets, 1939-45*. Methuen (Magnum Books), London, 1977
—— *Up the Line to Death: The War Poets, 1914-18*. Methuen, London, 1964
Graves, Robert. *Goodbye to All That*. Penguin, Harmondsworth, 1969
Greenwood, Walter. *Love On the Dole*. Penguin, Harmondsworth, 1969
Hillary, Richard. *The Last Enemy*. Pan, London, 1969
Hughes, Ted. *Crow*. Faber (paperback), London, 1974
Huxley, Aldous. *Antic Hay*. Penguin, Harmondsworth, 1969
Isherwood, Christopher. *Goodbye to Berlin and Other Stories*. Panther, St Albans, 1977
Kipling, Rudyard. *Kim*. Macmillan (paperback), London, 1961
—— *Verse*, Hodder and Stoughton, London, 1940
Larkin, Philip. *The North Ship*. Faber (paperback), London, 1974
Lawrence, D. H. *The Rainbow*. Penguin, Harmondsworth, 1969
Lewis, Alan. *In the Green Tree*. Allen and Unwin, London, 1949
MacNeice, Louis. *Collected Poems*. Faber, London, 1966
Mitchell, Hannah. *The Hard Way Up: The Autobiography of Hannah Mitchell, Suffragette and Rebel*. Virago (paperback), London, 1977
Morrell, Lady Ottoline. *Ottoline at Garsington: Memoirs of Lady Ottoline Morrell, 1915-18*. Edited by Robert Gathorne-Hardy. Faber, London, 1974
Naipaul, V. S. *Guerillas*. Penguin, Harmondsworth, 1976
Orwell, George. *The Collected Essays, Journalism and Letters of George Orwell*. (4 vols). Penguin, Harmondsworth, 1970
Plath, Sylvia. *Ariel*. Faber (paperback), London, 1968
Porter, Peter. *The Cost of Seriousness*. Oxford University Press, Oxford, 1978
Powell, Anthony. *A Dance to the Music of Time*. (12 vols). Collins (Fontana) London, 1967-77
Raine, Kathleen. *The Lost Country*. Hamish Hamilton, London, 1971
Roberts, Michael (Ed.). *New Signatures*. Hogarth Press, London, 1932
—— *New Country*. Hogarth Press, London, 1933
Sassoon, Siegfried. *Collected Poems 1908-56*. Faber, London, 1961

—— *Memoirs of an Infantry Officer*. Faber (paperback), London, 1965
—— *Siegfried's Journey 1916–20*. White Lion, London, 1973
Sitwell, Edith. *Selected Poems*. Macmillan (paperback), London, 1965
Smith, Stevie. *Collected Poems*. Allen Lane, Harmondsworth, 1975
Waugh, Evelyn. *Put Out More Flags*. Penguin, Harmondsworth, 1969
Wells, H. G. *The History of Mr Polly*. Pan, London, 1963
—— *Kipps*. Longmans, London, 1970
—— *Mr Britling Sees it Through*. Howard Baker, London, 1970
West, Rebecca. *A Celebration*. Macmillan, London, 1977
West, Vita Sackville. *The Edwardians*. Hogarth Press, London, 1960
Woolf, Virginia. *A Room of One's Own*. Panther, St Albans, 1977
Yeats, W. B. *Collected Poems*. Macmillan, London, 1950

3. FICTION FOR THE SAME AGE GROUP

Ballard, Martin. *Dockie*. Collins (Armada Lions), London, 1974
Banks, Lynne Reid. *The L-Shaped Room*. Penguin (Peacock), Harmondsworth, 1978
Bawden, Nina. *Carrie's War*. Penguin (Puffin), Harmondsworth, 1974
Darke, Marjorie. *A Question of Courage*. Kestrel, London, 1975
Garnett, Eve. *The Family from One End Street*. Penguin (Puffin), Harmondsworth, 1971
Grice, Frederick. *Nine Days Wonder*. Oxford University Press, London, 1976
Hamley, Dennis. *Very Far From Here*. Granada (Dragon Books), St Albans, 1978
Hartley, L. P. *The Go-Between*. Penguin, Harmondsworth, 1970
Hay, Ian. *The First Hundred Thousand*. Corgi, London, 1976
Lingard, Joan. *The Twelfth Day of July*. Penguin (Puffin), Harmondsworth, 1973
Llewellyn, Richard *How Green Was My Valley*. New English Library, London, 1967
Macdonald, Shelagh. *No End To Yesterday*. André Deutsch, London, 1977
Nesbit, Edith. *The Railway Children*. Penguin (Puffin), Harmondsworth, 1969
Walsh, Jill Paton. *The Dolphin Crossing*. Penguin (Puffin), Harmondsworth, 1970
Westall, Robert. *The Machine-gunners*. Penguin (Puffin), Harmondsworth, 1977

INDEX